THE BEATLES'
LIVERPOOL

Ron Jones

Liverpool History Press

Liverpool History Press

www.liverpoolhistorypress.co.uk

This book is dedicated to the memory of my parents
Charles and Frances Jones

The author would like to thank Mark Lewisohn for his invaluable help in verifying certain information in this guidebook and Pami Deol for assisting with the design and artwork.

First published in Great Britain in 1991 by Ron Jones Associates.

This Liverpool History Press edition published January 2014.

ISBN 978-0-9573833-2-6

Written by Ron Jones.

Published by the Liverpool History Press (an imprint of Ron Jones Associates Ltd).

Email: ron@rja-mpl.com

www.liverpoolhistorypress.co.uk

Printed and bound in China.

For Liverpool…
Birthplace of The Beatles

There are places I'll remember all my life,
Though some have changed,
Some forever, not for better,
Some have gone and some remain.

All these places had their moments,
With lovers and friends I still can recall,
Some are dead and some are living,
In my life I've loved them all.

In My Life by John Lennon and Paul McCartney.

3

Liddypool
('Liverpool' by John Lennon)

This visitor's guide to 'Liddypool' (Liverpool) by John Lennon was published in his book *In His Own Write*, although it first appeared in the *Mersey Beat* newspaper:

> "Reviving the old tradition of Judro Bathing is slowly but slowly dancing in Liddypool once more. Had you remembering these owld custard of Boldy Street blowing? The Peer Hat is very popularce for sun eating and Boots for Nude Brighter is handys when sailing. We are not happy with Queen Victorious Monologue, but Walky Through Gallery is goodly when the rain and Sit Georgie House is black (and white from the little pilgrims flying from Hellsy College). Talk Hall is very histerical with old things wot are fakes and King Anne never slept there I tell you. Shout Airborne is handly for planes if you like (no longer government patrolled) and the L.C.C.C. (Liddypool Cha Cha Cha) are doing a great thing. The Mersey Boat is selling another three copies to some go home foreigners who went home.
>
> There is a lot to do in Liddypool, but not all convenience."

But what does it all mean? As Paul McCartney said in the introduction to John's book…"None of it has to make sense, and if it seems funny then that's enough."

Here's my interpretation although I haven't a clue what his first sentence means!

> Can you remember the old custom of Bold Street blowing? The Pier Head is very popular for sun bathing and boats are handy for sailing to New Brighton. We are not happy with the Queen Victoria Monument, but the Walker Art Gallery is good when it's raining and St George's Hall is black (and white from the little pigeons). Speke Hall is very historical with old things that are fakes and I can tell you that Queen Anne never slept there. Speke Airport is handy if you like planes (it's no longer government controlled) and Liverpool City Council are doing a great job. The 'Mersey Beat' is selling another three copies to some "Go home foreigners!" who went home.
>
> There is a lot to do in Liverpool, but not all of it is convenient.

"Who knows why The Beatles happened? It's like the constant search for why you go down one road or why you go down another. It has as much to do with being from Liverpool, or being from Quarry Bank grammar school or being in a household where the library was full of Oscar Wilde and Whistler and Fitzgerald and all the Book of the Month Club." John

"…this is Liverpool. It is my husband John's birthplace and the place that he never stopped talking about all his life". Yoko Ono

Contents

Birthplace of The Beatles   6

Here, There and Everywhere:
Liverpool City Centre Beatle Trail   7-48

Magical History Tour:
South Liverpool   50-77
North and East Liverpool   78-84

Baby you can drive my car:
Beatle places in Wirral   86-91

The Beatles played here:
Merseyside venues played by The Beatles   92-95

Beatle Sights:
The top 20 Beatle heritage sights   96

Lennon's Liverpool:
Top 10 sights   97

In the town where I was born
Songs etc, influenced by Liverpool   98-106

Indexes   108-111

Image Credits   112

Maps:
In The Footsteps of The Beatles City Centre Trail   Inside front cover
Liverpool City Centre Beatles Trail   8/9
Cavern Quarter   42
South Liverpool   50
North and East Liverpool   78
Wirral / Merseyside   86
Liverpool City Centre Visitor Map   Inside back cover

The year is 1961. The Cuban heels of your winklepicker shoes clack noisily on the wet cobblestones. You turn up the collar on your short 'bum freezer' jacket to keep out the cold November wind that whips through this narrow canyon of a street flanked by age-blackened warehouses.

Light, and sound, spill from an open doorway. You head towards it. Excitement grips your stomach. You edge past the bulky frame of doorman Paddy Delaney who nods approval at the membership card held up for inspection. Carefully, for they are worn and steep, you descend, with quickening heartbeat, the 18 stone steps into the blackness below.

As you reach the bottom, it hits you like a sledgehammer. The wall of heat given off by a multitude of perspiring bodies. That odour, a mixture of cheap disinfectant, sweat, cigarette smoke and the mustiness of ancient cellars. The catacomb darkness pierced by a few naked light bulbs.

And the sound. Especially the sound. That all-consuming sound that sears the brain. The driving rhythm hacked out on the Rickenbacker, the melody robustly overlaid by the Gretsch. Underpinning it, the booming Hofner violin bass and, binding it all together, the unrelenting beat punched out on the drums.

You elbow a pathway through to the centre of the three aisles and look over the sea of bobbing heads, willing your eyes to cut through the fug to see who is producing that unique, exciting sound. As if confirmation were necessary. It could only come from one source.

Four figures clad in worn black leathers and sweat-sodden tee-shirts dominate the tiny wooden stage which threatens to shatter beneath the sheer power of the beat that is their hallmark. All eyes are fixed on the lead singer. Legs apart, hunched over his Rickenbacker, the microphone is but a whisper away from his lips. Through tortured vocal cords comes a raw sound which, despite the inferno-like heat, causes you to shiver... "You make me dizzy Miss Lizzy, with your rock and roll..."

Yes. This is the Cavern, Mathew Street. On stage is the greatest rock and roll band the world has ever known...The Beatles!

And this is Liverpool, 'City of The Beatles' YEAH! YEAH! YEAH!

Pier Head, Liverpool 1961

WALKING IN THE FOOTSTEPS OF THE BEATLES IN LIVERPOOL CITY CENTRE

The pages that follow set out a grand Liverpool City Centre Beatles trail. All of the important Beatle places and most of the tourist sights in the City Centre are included on this walk. Coincidentally, the trail takes you through parts of the city centre which were designated as a World Heritage Site in 2004.

Not allowing for any stops, it should take you about two hours to follow this trail. I suggest that you start at the Albert Dock where there are parking facilities, toilets and lots of eating and drinking places. Added to that it's Liverpool's top visitor attraction, home to The Beatles Story and a starting point for the Magical Mystery Bus Tour (see p10). What more could you possibly want?! The trail starts at the The Beatles Story and ends in Mathew Street (see pages 42-48). If it's more convenient, you could start there and finish at Albert Dock – simply follow the trail in reverse order.

Don't forget your camera; there are lots of interesting Beatle landmarks and great views of the city to photograph. Happy walking!

HELP!

Please respect the privacy of the people who live in the houses mentioned in these Beatles trails. Don't disturb them by knocking on their doors, peeping through their windows or otherwise trespassing on their property. The Beatles left Liverpool long ago and none of their families now live in any of these houses.

Care has been taken to ensure that the information in this book is correct. However, Liverpool is a restless, changing city. Many of the Beatle places featured in the first edition of this book, published in 1991, either don't exist now or have changed radically. The process continues unabated, one of the latest casualties being the former premises of NEMS, Whitechapel, the record store and management offices run by the Beatles' Manager, Brian Epstein, which was unceremoniously bulldozed in February 2012 to make way for (yet another) clothing store – see page 40.

Liverpool City Centre

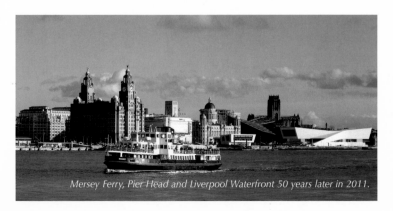

Mersey Ferry, Pier Head and Liverpool Waterfront 50 years later in 2011.

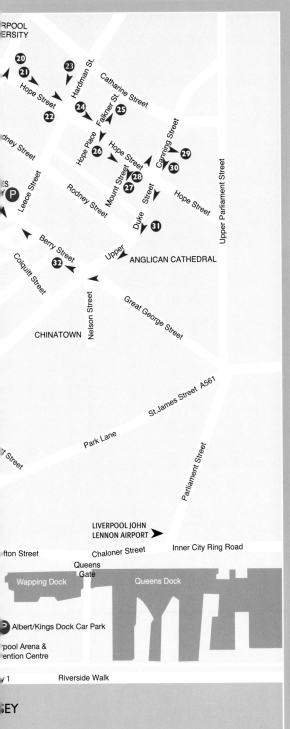

IN THE FOOTSTEPS OF THE BEATLES

LIVERPOOL CITY CENTRE

1. Albert Dock/Beatles Story 1
2. Mersey Ferries/Beatles Story 2
3. Liverpool Town Hall
4. Former Cassanova Club 1
5. Former Iron Door Club
6. St John's Gardens
7. Picton Library
8. Walker Art Gallery
9. Former Odeon Cinema
10. Former Cassanova Club 2
11. Empire Theatre
12. St George's Hall
13. Lime Street Train Station
14. Former Blacklers Store
15. Adelphi Hotel
16. Former Lewis's Store
17. 64 Mount Pleasant
18. 4 Rodney Street
19. R.C. Cathedral
20. Former Maternity Hospital
21. Former Everyman Theatre
22. Philharmonic Pub
23. Former Children's Hospital
24. Philharmonic Hall
25. 36 Falkner Street
26. Ye Cracke Pub
27. Former Liverpool Institute
28. Former College of Art
29. 7 Percy Street
30. 3 Gambier Terrace
31. Liverpool Cathedral
32. Blue Angel Club
33. Former Mersey Beat Office
34. Bold Street
35. Jacaranda Club
36. Epstein Theatre
37. Former Reece's Restaurant
38. Bluecoat Chambers
39. Former NEMS
40. Former Rushworth's Music
41. Former Hessy's Music Store
42. Cavern Quarter–see pp42-48

9

STARTING POINT: THE BEATLES STORY / ALBERT DOCK

No visitor to Liverpool should leave the city without visiting the Albert Dock, and not just because it is home to The Beatles Story, the city's one and only Beatles 'museum'. The converted warehouses, dating from 1846, form the largest group of Grade One 'listed' buildings (on account of their historical and architectural importance) in Britain. The complex, a mixture of shops, restaurants and bars, hotels, top-class visitor attractions, luxury apartments and offices, is the most popular free heritage attraction in the country, pulling in over four million visitors a year. The Albert Dock is visually stunning and a very pleasant place in which to spend the day.

In the basement of Britannia Pavilion is **The Beatles Story** which opened in 1990. The Beatles Story is literally that...the story of The Beatles from their childhood days through to their break-up and the pursuit of individual careers. This is done by way of a series of rooms including the office of the Mersey Beat newspaper, Hamburg's Reeperbahn, the Cavern, the Yellow Submarine, a Lennon 'White Room' etc. There is also a large souvenir shop which is open daily from 10am. A replica of the Casbah Coffee Club was added in 1999 (see also pp81-83).

An extension, opened in 2008, effectively doubled the size of The Beatles Story. The gallery, *Going Solo,* focuses on the individual Beatles' solo careers and a special exhibition space stages a changing programme of themed exhibitions. A hands-on, inter-active Discovery Zone will be of special interest to families and school groups. Creature comforts are catered for in the Starbucks Café and chill-out area whilst a large Fab4Store completes the visitor experience.

To get the most out of your visit, opt for the "Living History" tour, narrated by John Lennon's half-sister Julia. You'll also hear the voices of Brian Epstein, Paul McCartney, Allan Williams, Cynthia Lennon and George Martin as they tell you about the group's rise to fame. The tour is available in eight languages. For the latest information, booking admission tickets on-line, browsing the

Above left: recreation of the Cavern Club in The Beatles Story. Above right: Memorabilia on display in 'The Beatles Love Me Do' special exhibition in the Museum of Liverpool.

on-line shop etc., check out - *www.beatlesstory.com*

To the immediate right of the Beatles Story is the main entrance to Albert Dock. Turn left onto the quayside and follow it round to **Tate Liverpool**. There are no Beatles connections but, if you have the time and modern art is your thing, it is well worth a visit. Good café, bookshop and toilets.

Across the Hartley Bridge, to the right, is the **Merseyside Maritime Museum** and **International Slavery Museum** both of which should be on your 'must visit' list, as should the brand new **Museum of Liverpool** – it's the strikingly modern white building staight ahead of you; head for the *Wondrous Place* gallery where you will find a special Beatles display of memorabilia, including stage suits worn by the Fab Four, a jacket that belonged to ousted Beatle, Pete Best, and a re-creation of John and Yoko's 1969 Amsterdam 'bed-in' stunt. There's also a short audio-visual Beatles Show in a small theatre which boasts the actual stage from St Peter's Church Hall where John and Paul met and played together for the very first time on 6th July 1957 – see page 70.

Admission to all three museums is free. The same is true for Tate Liverpool but expect to pay an admission charge for their special exhibitions.

Kings Dock, immediately south of the Albert Dock, was the setting for a fabulous *Let It Be Liverpool* open air concert staged by Paul on the evening of 28th June 1990. He was back again here on 1st June 2003 to perform the final gig of his world tour. Once a car park, the site is now the home of the new Liverpool Echo Arena and BT Convention Centre. On 12th January 2008 Ringo and a host of other local musical luminaries took part in the opening event – *Liverpool - The Musical*. Paul also played a gig there on 20 December 2011, shortly after his marriage to American heiress Nancy Shevell.

(Leave Albert Dock by crossing the footbridge over the entrance to the dock and head towards the Museum of Liverpool and the Pier Head.)

THE PIER HEAD / MERSEY FERRIES

Departure point for the famous Mersey Ferries, and nowadays cruise liners. The Pier Head and its landmark buildings, the Pier Head group. The Cunard Building, Port of Liverpool Building, and especially the Royal Liver Building topped by the mythical twin Liver Birds, are powerful emotive symbols of the city for all *Liverpudlians*, or *Scousers* as we are sometimes called.

It has always been an especially favourite place for Liverpool children and The Beatles were no exception. They would be drawn here to marvel at the giant transatlantic liners which were such a glamorous feature of the Pier Head until the early 1970's. A Cruise Liner Terminal, opened in 2007, has seen increasing numbers of cruise-ships including Liverpool in their itineraries. No doubt The Beatles also rode on the now-demolished Overhead Electric Railway, the world's first, and nick-named *The Docker's Umbrella*, which gave them a bird's eye view of the then booming Liverpool docks stretching from Dingle in the south, near Ringo's home, to Seaforth in the north.

John, Paul, George and Ringo would travel here on bone-rattling *Green Goddesses*, Liverpool's much-missed electric trams, to catch the ferryboats that would take them across the fast-flowing River Mersey to the funfair and sands at New Brighton or the beaches at Wallasey.

Royal Iris

The ferry to New Brighton has long gone but you can still savour one of the truly essential Liverpool experiences – a short trip on one of the famous old Mersey Ferries, built at the beginning of the 1960's. The ferries are immortalised in the Gerry and the Pacemakers song *Ferry 'cross the Mersey* which, along with their other hit *You'll never walk alone* have become twin anthems for Liverpool.

Launched in 1951, the *Royal Iris* had been the most high profile of the Mersey Ferries 'fleet' for some 40 years. Intended as an up-market dance-cruise ship, she became known to one and all as the 'fish and chip boat'. It was as such that The Beatles performed on board her during 1961 and 1962 in five *Riverboat Shuffles* presented by the Cavern. Judged too expensive to repair, she was eventually pensioned off.

The Pier Head was also the venue for a controversial Lennon concert on 5th May 1990 promoted by Yoko Ono who appeared on stage with Sean and a host of pop luminaries. Performers as diverse as Lou Reed, Cyndi

Lauper, Randy Travis and Kylie Mynogue performed cover versions of Lennon hits. The event did raise more than £300,000 to enable the University of Liverpool to set up a scholarship fund to help needy students. A video of the concert *Lennon: A Tribute* was released in April 1991.

A new Mersey Ferries terminal, opened in 2009, houses a Beatles Story Fab4D attraction and an exhibition to complement the one at Albert Dock.

(Turn right at the statue of King Edward VII on horseback and go between the Royal Liver and Cunard Buildings. At the traffic lights, cross the dock road into Water Street. At the top of Water Street, jutting out into the road, is Liverpool Town Hall)

LIVERPOOL TOWN HALL *Water Street*
BEATLES' CIVIC RECEPTION

As they stood on the balcony (pictured right) along-side the Lord Mayor and other civic dignitaries, The Beatles received a hero's welcome from the tens of thousands of their Merseyside fans who crowded the streets fanning out from the Town Hall.

Earlier on that Friday evening, 10 July 1964, they had headed a cavalcade cheered by nearly a quarter of a million fans as it slowly made its way from Speke Airport to the city centre and the glittering civic reception that awaited them.

From the Minstrel's Gallery, The Beatles gazed down on the specially invited guests assembled to pay homage to them in the ballroom of the City's beautiful Georgian Town Hall, built in 1754. Earlier, in the intimacy of the Lord Mayor's Parlour, they had sipped tea from china cups elegantly embossed with the city's Coat of Arms.

Later that evening, to yet more scenes of Beatlemania, they attended the northern premiere of their first film *A Hard Day's Night* at the Odeon Cinema in London Road. They had well and truly 'arrived' in Liverpool the city of their birth.

In the Council Chamber on the ground floor the City Council passed the resolution that confirmed the honour of *Freemen of the City* on The Beatles. Their names are inscribed on the list of Honorary Freemen in the Entrance Hall. Public openings are arranged in August every year. A visit is highly recommended.

(Continue along Dale Street. Cross the lights at North John Street. On the next block is The Temple)

Liverpool City Centre

CASSANOVA CLUB *The Temple, Dale Street*

Named after popular Merseybeat group, Cass and the Cassanovas, the Cassanova Club was housed for a short time in an upstairs room in the Temple building. Here on a Sunday afternoon early in 1960 The Beatles played during the interval.

(Turn into Temple Street to the new office building half way down the street on the left.)

THE IRON DOOR *13 Temple Street, off Dale Street*

The bronze plaque on the wall of 5 Temple Square commemorates the fact that the 19th century warehouse that once stood here was the home of the famous beat club, The Iron Door was initially opened by Geoff Hogarth as a jazz club on 9th April 1960. Eleven months later, in March 1961 when it was still known as the Liverpool Jazz Society, The Beatles played five gigs here.

In a sense, The Iron Door is Merseybeat's 'forgotten club' yet it is worth making the point that it pre-dates the Cavern as a rock and roll venue and perhaps merits its title of 'The Cradle of Merseybeat'. The Iron Door was the venue on 11th March 1961 for Merseyside's first 'all-nighter' staged by pioneering local rock and roll promoter Sam Leach – 12 bands played for 12 hours from 8pm on the Saturday night until 8am on Sunday morning. Mike Jackson, drummer with the Mojos, remembers stepping over a body in the cloakrooms here early one Sunday morning - it was John Lennon having a sleep. "Cold in here. isn't it?" he said, pulling the coat that served as a blanket closer to him.

The plaque names The Beatles and 14 other bands, including Kingsize Taylor and the Dominos whose leader, Teddy Taylor, performed the unveiling.

(At the bottom of Temple Street turn left into Victoria Street. Continue to the end of the street and cross the road to St John's Gardens at the rear of St George's Hall)

ST JOHN'S GARDENS

In the Peace Garden, near the rear of St George's Hall, a tree in memory of John Lennon, was planted in 2000 by his half-sister, Julia. Four days after his death on 3 December 2001, an English oak tree in memory of George Harrison was planted on the opposite side of the Gardens between an Indian bean tree and the *Tree of Life*, appropriate given George's interests in horticulture, India and mysticism. The trees are unmarked, making it impossible for visitors to locate them.

(At the top left-hand exit, enter William Brown Street. This is the cultural heart of the city centre with its World Museum Liverpool, libraries complex, Walker Art Gallery and St George's Hall.)

William Brown Street. The Picton Library is the round building on the left. The building below is the Walker Art Gallery.

PICTON LIBRARY *William Brown Street*
PAUL'S 'FREEDOM OF THE CITY' CEREMONY

Lamentably, any proposal to honour Liverpool's most famous sons created discord in the city of their birth: 'twas ever thus. Nevertheless, on 7 March 1984, Liverpool City Council managed to pass a resolution bestowing on each Beatle the Honorary Freedom of the City, the highest honour it is possible for an individual to receive from the City. Passing a resolution was one thing. Getting The Beatles to come to Liverpool to be formally made Freemen of the City was something else. Yoko finally collected John's Freedom of the City award in a tree-planting ceremony in New York's Strawberry Field in October 1998. George and Ringo's scrolls are still locked away in the City Council's safe awaiting collection!

Always the most amenable and public relations conscious of the Fab Four, Paul readily accepted the invitation. And it was in this impressive circular domed library that, on 28 November 1984, Paul McCartney MBE received the scroll which confirmed his new status as a Freeman of the City.

At that time the infamous Militant-controlled Council was steering the City towards bankruptcy. "Does this mean I get to see the books?" Paul joked as he responded to speeches by Council worthies.

Among items of Beatle interest held by the library (but rarely on display) are the baptism records of George and Ringo and a programme for the Woolton Village fete held on 6th July 1957 – when Paul and John met for the first time. *The Library is closed until 2013 whilst it undergoes a £50m redevelopment.*

(Next door to the Picton Library is the Walker Art Gallery)

WALKER ART GALLERY *William Brown Street*

One of Stuart Sutcliffe's paintings was selected from amongst thousands of entries for the prestigious bi-annual John Moores Liverpool Exhibition held here in 1959. Moores, founder of the once-famous Littlewoods football pools, catalogue and High Street stores empire, and after whom one of the city's three universities, the Liverpool John Moores University is named, bought the painting for £65 for his private collection. For the struggling art student it was in those days a princely sum. Stu promptly spent part of it on a down-payment for an electric bass guitar enabling him to join John, Paul and George.

15

When he was 21 Stu died of a brain haemorrhage in the arms of his German fiance Astrid Kirchherr. He had been studying under Eduardo Paolozzi at the Hamburg College of Art. Two years later, in 1964, with Beatlemania at its height, his mother persuaded the Walker to stage an exhibition of his work. It ran from 2nd to 24th May and was seen by over 11,000 visitors.

One of Stu's paintings, 'Hamburg Painting No.2', is owned by the Walker and is normally on view. Pictured (*right*) is another of Stu's *Hamburg* paintings, displayed in *The Art of The Beatles* exhibition.

In 1983 I was asked to come up with ideas for how places like the Walker Art Gallery could celebrate Liverpool's International Garden Festival Year and generally make themselves more interesting to visit in 1984. Thus was born the concept of *The Art of The Beatles* exhibition. Fellow Beatle project collaborator Mike Evans and I put together an exhibition which was sniffily accepted by the Gallery. It ran from May to September 1984, attracted nearly 50,000 paying visitors and was judged a great success. The fans certainly loved it! Paul contributed the drumskin for the Peter Blake *Sgt Pepper* album cover collage below.

Cynthia Lennon accepted our invitation to open the exhibition and related the times when she and John, as awestruck art students, would tip toe round the Walker speaking in whispers. He would have seen the funny side of *The Art of The Beatles* show. By the Walker's standards, it was slightly irreverent – there was non-stop Beatle music and videos, a pile of bricks from the old Cavern (shades of the Tate!) and the hallowed walls displayed his once-banned 'Bag One' drawings alongside paintings from his childhood. The exhibition later toured Japan and was also staged in Cologne.

"John and I spent many a pleasant afternoon wandering around the Walker when we were young, so going back to the 'Pool with my paintings will complete some kind of circle for me and I'm really excited about it" said Paul when the first comprehensive exhibition of his paintings in Britain, was staged here in 2002. The 60 plus paintings, sculpture and photo pieces that made up 'the art of Paul McCartney' drew comments from critics which varied from "truly surprising" to "a dog's dinner of dreadful dawbs defying description". But Her Majesty the Queen, who was given a private tour of the exhibition by 'her knight', Sir Paul, was quite taken by it: "Very colourful." she enthused.

(At the top of William Brown Street, cross Lime Street to the Empire Theatre on the corner of London Road and Lime Street. On the next block up London Road is the former Odeon Cinema.)

FORMER ODEON CINEMA *London Road*

Before it was split into a number of smaller cinemas, the Odeon was one enormous 'picture palace'. On 7th December 1963 it was the venue for two performances by The Beatles following a hectic afternoon at the nearby Empire Theatre.

On 10th July 1964, the same day that The Beatles had been honoured at a civic reception at Liverpool Town Hall, the Odeon became the setting for the northern premiere of The Beatles' first film *A Hard Day's Night*. It was a Hollywood-style event easily surpassing the film's earlier Royal premiere in London. The 1969 film, *The Magic Christian*, in which Ringo co-starred with Peter Sellers, was also given its northern premiere here.

Another glittering event took place here on the evening of 28th November 1984 when Paul and Linda McCartney attended the UK premiere of Paul's film *Give My Regards To Broad Street.* During the afternoon Paul had been made an Honorary Freeman of the City of Liverpool. The Odeon held early memories for Paul: he had paid 24 shillings to watch Bill Haley and the Comets perform live here in 1957. The film *Backbeat*, which told the story of The Beatles' early days, was given its world premiere here on 24 March 1994.

Opened in 1934 as the Paramount, the Odeon finally closed in October 2008. It has since been demolished and is currently a temporary car park.

(Opposite here, above the old storefronts, was the former Cassanova Club.)

CASSANOVA CLUB / PEPPERMINT LOUNGE *London Rd/Fraser St.*

The Cassanova Club transferred to Sampson and Barlow's ballroom here from its short-lived home in The Temple, Dale Street, and was opened by local promoter Sam Leach on 9th February 1961. Two days later The Beatles played the first of seven dates here.

The following week, on Valentine's night, fans paid four shillings and sixpence (about 22 pence – refreshments included!) to bop to The Beatles, the Big Three, Rory Storm and the Hurricanes and Mark Peters and the Cyclones. The Cassanova Club hit the headlines 35 years later when the first-ever film footage of The Beatles – half a minute of colour film without sound, reputedly shot in the club on that very night – came to light.

Later, as the Peppermint Lounge, or 'The Pep' as it was known, it continued to be a popular venue for local groups although by then The Beatles had moved on.

Further down Fraser Street was Mr Pickwick's club, the setting for the first-ever Liverpool Beatles Convention on 8/9th October 1977, masterminded by Cavern DJ Bob Wooler and Beatles' manager Allan Williams. My role was to persuade the English Tourist Board to fund the event. It was my first involvement with Bob and Allan and turned out to be quite an experience!

(Return to Lime Street.)

EMPIRE THEATRE *Lime Street*

The City's biggest and most glamourous theatre where, on 9th June 1957, the Quarry Men competed against other local hopefuls for the chance to appear on Carroll 'Mr Star-Maker' Levis's TV show. They failed this audition but were more successful when, as Johnny and the Moondogs, they competed here three times in October 1959, winning a place in the final round of auditions in Manchester.

Two weeks later, with the prospect of fame and fortune within their sights, John, Paul and George came back to Lime Street on the train from Manchester with their tails between their legs. The auditions had run on late into the evening. They didn't have the money to stay in Manchester overnight so they had to come home before it was their turn to audition.

When they returned to play the Empire again on 28th October 1962 The Beatles had really hit the big time in the eyes of their Liverpool fans, even though they took second billing to Little Richard, Craig Douglas, Kenny Lynch, Sounds Incorporated and Jet Harris.

The Beatles stood in the shower of their cramped dressing room at the Empire Theatre for this photograph.

Over the next two years The Beatles were to appear here on another six occasions two of which were especially memorable. On the afternoon of 7th December 1963, they gave a special concert for 2,500 members of their Northern Area Fan Club and took part in the filming of Juke Box Jury to the added delight of those same fans. That evening, as The Beatles gave two concerts at the Odeon cinema round the corner from the Empire, 23 million television viewers saw the unique 'Juke Box Jury' panel of John, Paul, George and Ringo pass judgement on a batch of the latest record releases.

Paul came on stage here at the end of the 'A Concert For George' tribute on 24th February 2002, reminisced about his old friend and sang 'Yesterday'.

The Beatles' 11th and final appearance at the Empire took place on 5th December 1965. Little did their adoring army of local fans realise that it was also to be the very last time their idols were to perform in Liverpool as a group. However, George was back on stage here in 1969 with Delaney & Bonnie, Paul played here in 1973 and again in 1975 with his band Wings. And Ringo with his All Starr Band, featuring son Zak also on drums, was here in 1992.

(Directly opposite the Empire is St George's Hall.)

ST. GEORGE'S HALL *Lime Street*

Completed in 1854, St George's Hall is ranked as one of the finest Graeco-Roman style buildings in the world and is a fitting memorial to its 23 year-old architect, Harvey Lonsdale Elmes –a visit is highly recommended.

On 13th May 1960 this was the setting for a wild Liverpool Arts Ball, organised by Allan Williams and based on the famous Chelsea Arts Ball. He commissioned The Beatles to design and make decorative floats – one was in the shape of a guitar – which were destined to be destroyed by the revellers during the course of the evening. The ball ended in chaos with the hall's outraged owners, Liverpool City Council, swearing "never again". But memories are short and they allowed the 1984 Beatles Convention to take place here, this time without incident.

On the Sunday following John's murder, tens of thousands of still-grieving fans held an emotional vigil on the plateau in front of the hall where, two decades earlier, along with Paul and George and fellow art student Stu Sutcliffe, he had struggled with their carnival floats. The crowds were back on the plateau again for a candlelit vigil on 3rd December 2001 to mark the untimely death of George Harrison three days earlier.

More recently, on 11th January 2008, Ringo was the star turn at the launch of Liverpool's reign as 'European Capital of Culture'. Tens of thousands watched as he performed the title song of his new album *Liverpool 8* from the roof of St George's Hall.

(Continue along Lime Street)

LIME STREET TRAIN STATION

"Oh Maggie Maggie May, they have taken her away and she'll never walk down Lime Street any more." sang John in The Beatles' version of the famous Liverpool folk song *Maggie May*. A place of many Beatle comings and goings in the early 60's; more particularly, Brian Epstein made frequent trips to London in a vain attempt to interest record companies in The Beatles...until, in June 1962, they auditioned for EMI in the form of George Martin.

(Look across the road to the left where you will see the Royal Court Theatre, Roe Street. The Beatles never performed there but in November 1979 Wings played four nights on the run, the first gig being an exclusive free concert given by Paul for masters and pupils from his old school, the Liverpool Institute. Julian Lennon also performed here in 1989. Continue along Lime Street to its junction with Elliot Street. Look to the left and you will see Weatherspoons, formerly Blacklers store.)

FORMER BLACKLERS STORE *Great Charlotte Street/Elliot Street*

In between leaving school and joining the Silver Beetles on their tour of Scotland with Johnny Gentle in 1960, George Harrison served a brief apprenticeship here as an electrician – "I got a job cleaning all the lights with a paint brush, all those tubes to keep clean, and at Christmas I kept the Grotto clean."

NEMS opened their first city centre branch in Great Charlotte Street in the late 1950's. Brian Epstein ran the record section with military precision and made such a success of it that his father was quickly encouraged to open another, bigger, store in Whitechapel.

(Continue along Lime Street.)

Wonder if George had to keep these giant light fittings clean too? Blacklers was a Liverpool institution and its mention is guaranteed to make the eyes of older Liverpudlians mist over.

BRITANNIA ADELPHI HOTEL *Ranelagh Place*

Built during the days when Liverpool was the country's premier port for trans-atlantic passengers, the Adelphi is the last remaining big old Liverpool hotel.

It is the magnificent setting for the annual Beatles Convention held at the end of August every year and attended by fans from all over the world. The American conventions are bigger and slicker affairs but the Liverpool event has that extra special ingredient that can't be found anywhere else in the world – after all, it is held 'In the town where they were born'!

The Beatles never stayed at the Adelphi but Yoko and Sean stopped off here in 1990 when they were in Liverpool for John's memorial concert at the Pier Head. The hotel achieved nationwide notoriety in 1997 as the subject of the warts-and-all documentary series *Hotel* which portrayed it in a poor light.

(Look across the street to Lewis's store opposite)

FORMER LEWIS'S STORE *Ranalegh Street*

The top floor of this former iconic department store was the setting for a Beatles performance at a staff 'Young Idea Dance' for the '527 Club' on 28th November 1962. And, for a short time, Paul even worked as a 'second man' on one of the store's vans.

John and Cynthia regularly met under the store's dramatic statue (right) of a naked man arms reaching heavenward. This once-controversial figure (known to many Liverpudlians, for obvious reasons, as 'Dickie Lewis') represents 'Liverpool Resurgent' and was sculpted by Epstein – Jacob, not Brian! After 154 years, Lewis's finally closed in 2010; the building is to be incorporated into a £200m 'Central Village' redevelopment scheme.

(Cross at the traffic lights and continue up the right hand side of Mount Pleasant)

FORMER REGISTRY OFFICE *64 Mount Pleasant*
JOHN AND CYNTHIA'S WEDDING

On Thursday 23rd August 1962 a strange little ceremony was performed here, a former Georgian town house built in 1773. The participants were John, Paul, George, Brian Epstein and Cynthia and her brother and his wife. The occasion? The marriage of Beatle John to his pregnant art school girlfriend Cynthia Powell. The brief ceremony was conducted to the ear-splitting accompaniment of a pneumatic drill operated by a workman in the building next door. Ringo wasn't there. He'd only just joined The Beatles and hadn't been invited; John didn't even tell him he'd got married that day!

After the brief ceremony, they had all sprinted down the hill in the pouring rain to queue in Reece's restaurant for the wedding breakfast. John spent his wedding night playing a gig with The Beatles in Chester! There was to be no proper honeymoon either. The Beatles' crowded diary of engagements wouldn't allow it. It was a marriage destined not to last very long. Six years later, on 8th November 1968, it ended in the divorce court following John's admitted adultery with his 'soul-mate', the Japanese artist Yoko Ono.

In this same Registry Office 24 years earlier, on 3rd December 1938, John's mother Julia, a cinema usherette, had married ship's steward Freddie Lennon. The next day Freddie sailed off to the West Indies. Julia saw little of him during their brief and stormy marriage and, by the time John was 18 months old, Freddie had left them both for good.

(Continue to the traffic lights at the junction of Mount Pleasant and Rodney Street. Just around the corner, on the right is No 4)

NO 4 RODNEY STREET - BRIAN EPSTEIN'S BIRTHPLACE

Elegantly Georgian, Rodney Street is Liverpool's equivalent of London's 'street of doctors', Harley Street. Number 4 was the home of James Maury. He was appointed as America's very first Consul in Great Britain by George Washington in 1790 and was U.S. Consul in Liverpool from that year until 1829. Of more interest to Beatle fans, it was once a private nursing home and the birthplace, on 19th September 1934, of Brian Samuel Epstein – pronounced 'Epsteen' but known to the Beatles and his other Merseybeat groups simply as 'Eppy'. To the staff of his NEMS records shops he was the more formal 'Mr Brian'.

His parents, Harry and Queenie, were prosperous middle-class Jews and were easily able to afford a live-in nanny for Brian at their very 'des res' (desirable residence) at the posh end of Queens Drive (see p61).

At the height of The Beatles' success a radio interviewer asked Brian – "Were you born in Liverpool?" He replied, "I would have said it was essential.", the clear inference being that he could not have steered The Beatles to fame and fortune had he not been a fellow Liverpudlian.

(Continue to the top of Mount Pleasant. The R. C. Cathedral is on the opposite side of the road; no Beatle connections but it is a modern classic and should definitely be visited.)

ROMAN CATHOLIC CATHEDRAL *Mount Pleasant*

Visitors to the R.C. Cathedral, or the Metropolitan Cathedral of Christ the King to give it its full title, either like it or they don't. From the outside it's a controversial building, architecturally, but reserve your judgement till you've looked inside. Most critics are stunned into silence.

Completed in 1967, it is known to irreverent Liverpudlians as 'Paddy's Wigwam' ('Paddy'? – The city has a large Irish Catholic population). It has also been nick-named 'The Mersey Funnel' and 'The Pope's Launching Pad'.

You'll also find a café, souvenir shop and toilets here.

(Cross the traffic lights at the junction of Mount Pleasant and Hope Street into Oxford Street. The next street along is Arrad Street. Keep to the left of the 'Font' bar and you will see the former Maternity Hospital, known to many older Liverpudlians as 'The Stork Hotel'. Closed in 1995, it has since been converted into apartments.)

FORMER OXFORD STREET MATERNITY HOSPITAL (now part of Unite Student Village), JOHN LENNON'S BIRTHPLACE

Here, in the old main building, at 6.30pm on Wednesday, the 9th October 1940, arguably Liverpool's most famous son, John Winston Lennon, was born. No memorial plaque was erected over his bed; nobody can even remember which ward he was born in! His Aunt Mimi favoured the name John and Winston was no doubt chosen as a patriotic tribute to Britain's great wartime leader Winston Churchill who was that very day elected leader of the Conservative Party.

On Saturday 12th October this notice of John's birth appeared in the Liverpool Echo:

> LENNON-October 9, in hospital to JULIA (nee Stanley), wife of ALFRED LENNON, Merchant Navy (at sea), a son-9 Newcastle Road.

John's own zany account of his birth, written for the *Mersey Beat* newspaper, is more interesting – "I was bored on the 9 October 1940, when, I believe, the Nasties were still booming us, led by Madalf Heatlump (who only had one). Anyway they didn't get me…"

Most accounts of John's birth tell of Aunt Mimi dodging shrapnel as she ran through the bomb-torn streets of Liverpool to see the new baby, who had to be placed under the bed during the air raid. It's a nice, whimsical, oft-told tale... but a tall one for all that. Official war records confirm that the Luftwaffe gave Liverpool a miss that particular night.

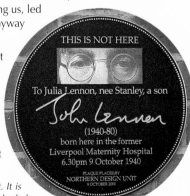

THIS IS NOT HERE

To Julia Lennon, nee Stanley, a son

John Lennon

(1940-80)
born here in the former
Liverpool Maternity Hospital
6.30pm 9 October 1940

PLAQUE PLACED BY
NORTHERN DESIGN UNIT
9 OCTOBER 2000

(Retrace your steps and turn left into Hope Street. It is neat that Liverpool can boast two world-class cathedrals, each at either end of a street called 'Hope'.)

EVERYMAN THEATRE
Hope Street

Although Merseybeat groups started to appear from late 1962, The Beatles never played here. However, it is known that George and Ringo came along to at least one of the poetry readings that were a feature of Liverpool's famous poetry scene in the 60's. "Liverpool is the centre of all human consciousness" – declared Allen Ginsberg, American poet and leading apostle of the beat generation at the time. Liverpudlians loved him for it even though they didn't have a clue what he was talking about. Nor did they

Liverpool actor Mark McGann played John in the hit production of the play 'Lennon'.

understand Carl Gustav Jung, the celebrated Swiss philosopher, when he pronounced, following a dream that changed his life, that "Liverpool is the Pool of Life."

More significantly, Paul turned 'performance poet' on 21 March 2001 when he gave a reading of some of the poems from his first anthology *Blackbird Singing* to an audience of 400 at this theatre. Earlier that day, some 3,000 fans had queued at W H Smith's bookshop in Church Street for a chance to meet Paul and buy a signed copy of *Blackbird Singing*.

The Everyman's real Beatle pedigree is to be found in the plays premiered here. *John, Paul, George, Ringo and Bert* by Liverpool playwright Willy Russell, of *Shirley Valentine, Educating Rita* and *Blood Brothers* fame, had its world premiere here in 1974. It played to capacity houses for six weeks before transferring to the West End of London and then, in 1982, off-Broadway, New York, where it received indifferent reviews.

This was followed in 1981 by the premiere of *Lennon*, a musical play devised and directed by Bob Eaton and *Sgt. Pepper's Magical Mystery Trip* premiered here in 1996.

The Everyman closed in Summer 2011 and will be replaced by a £28m 'New Everyman' Theatre in 2013.

(Continue along Hope Street to its junction with Hardman Street. On the opposite side of the road is one of John Lennon's favourite pubs, the 'Phil'.)

PHILHARMONIC PUB *Hope Street*

This, the best example of Victorian pub exuberance in a city full of fine pubs, was frequented by The Beatles as an alternative to their regular pub 'Ye Cracke' a short distance further along Hope Street. John later bemoaned the fact that the price of fame was…"not being able to go to the *Phil* for a drink".

The *Phil* is perhaps unique in allowing ladies to be given guided tours of the richly-marbled gents lavatories.

(Cross at the traffic lights to the Philharmonic Hall. If you look up Hardman Street you will see, on the opposite side of the road, the Liverpool Community College Arts Centre, built on the site of the Royal Liverpool Children's Hospital.)

ROYAL LIVERPOOL CHILDREN'S HOSPITAL *Myrtle Street.*
Demolished and replaced by Liverpool Community College's Arts Centre

When he was nearly seven years old Ringo was rushed here with violent stomach pains. His appendix had burst. Peritonitis set in and he slipped into a dangerous coma. He was not expected to survive that first night. Happily, he pulled through but recovery was slow and he remained here for about six months. Dogged by bad luck, he even managed to fall out of bed and open up the scars from his operation, just when he was about to return to his home in the nearby Dingle.

Illness struck Ringo down yet again when he was thirteen, this time with pleurisy. He was to spend another six months or so in the hospital's sanatorium (now demolished) at Heswall on the Wirral coast. It was there that he caught another bug...drumming.

His childhood friend and close neighbour Marie Maguire (now Marie Crawford and an official BeatleGuide) was a regular visitor to Heswall and remembers him as an enthusiastic member of the ward band. On one occasion she presented a delighted Ringo with Eric Delaney's record *Bedtime For Drums*. It was Marie who had taught the sickly Ringo, or 'Richy' as he was known to everyone in those days, to read and write. Illness had robbed him of even a basic education.

PHILHARMONIC HALL *Hope Street*

In common with most Liverpool school children, each member of The Beatles no doubt attended at least one concert at the 'Phil' by the RLPO (Royal Liverpool Philharmonic Orchestra) during the 50's.

From the late 50's it became a popular venue for pop groups, but not The Beatles. One of their early major influences, Buddy Holly and the Crickets, played here in 1958. The copyright to Holly's music is now owned by one of his biggest fans, Paul McCartney.

The by-now famous George was here again in 1963 as a panelist judging the final of the Lancashire and Cheshire Beat Group Competition. Also on the jury was Dick Rowe, forever remembered as 'the man who turned down the Beatles'. George had been impressed by a new R & B group he'd seen in London and suggested that Rowe should sign them up. The band?…the Rolling Stones. This time Rowe does the right thing and takes George's advice.

From time to time the hall echoes to orchestral versions of Beatles' classics, most notably when their recording manager George Martin, sometimes dubbed 'The Fifth Beatle', conducted the orchestra.

To celebrate the orchestra's 150th anniversary in 1991, Paul McCartney wrote a full-length orchestral symphony *Liverpool Oratorio* in collaboration with American-born composer Carl Davis. Although rehearsals took place here, the premiere was staged in the Anglican Cathedral on the 28th and 29th June. Fittingly, after being performed in twenty countries, the 100th performance took place here in September 1996 with the proud McCartney in attendance.

A pun on his 'working class' Liverpool roots, *Working Classical*, Paul's third orchestral work (the second was *Standing Stone*), performed by the London Symphony Orchestra with the Loma Mar Quartet, was premiered here on 16 October 1999. Paul and members of his family were in the audience. At around the same time, and in stark contrast to his late interest in orchestral and chamber music, Paul released *Run Devil Run*, comprised mainly of cover versions of rock and roll classics which influenced him as a teenager growing up in Liverpool in the 1950's.

The 1968 film *Yellow Submarine*, digitally enhanced and with a re-mixed soundtrack, was given its UK premier here on 14 September 1999 and, on the 2nd July 2001, Yoko Ono walked on stage to be made a Doctor of Laws by the University of Liverpool in recognition of her work as a conceptual artist and for the John Lennon Memorial Scholarship which she helped establish in 1991 to assist the higher education of needy students. Receiving her honorary degree she remarked - "You have no idea what this means to me, for this is not any city, this is Liverpool. It is my husband John's birthplace and the place that he never stopped talking about all his life."

(Continue along Hope Street and turn left into Falkner Street. No 36 is on the right hand side, near the far end of the street.)

NO 36 FALKNER STREET
JOHN AND CYNTHIA'S HONEYMOON FLAT

The Beatles' manager Brian Epstein rented, but hardly ever used, the ground floor flat of this house. When John and Cynthia got married in August 1962,

Brian let them honeymoon at the flat until they found a place of their own. Eventually, John and Cyn moved back to *Mendips* his Aunt Mimi's house in Menlove Avenue.

Whilst living here John had written *Do you want to know a secret?*, sung by George on the *Please, Please Me* album. It was also the song which had propelled another of Epstein's Merseybeat groups, Billy J Kramer and the Dakotas, to the top of the charts. John recalled the time he wrote the song:

"I was in the first apartment I'd ever had that wasn't shared by fourteen other students – gals and guys at art school. I'd just married Cyn and Brian Epstein gave us his secret little apartment that he kept in Liverpool for his sexual liaisons separate from his home life. And he let Cyn and I have that apartment."

(Re-trace your steps to Hope Street and cross over into Rice Street)

'YE CRACKE' *Rice Street*

The local pub for students from the nearby Art College and, occasionally, mature looking schoolboys from the Liverpool Institute. 'Black Velvets' would be drunk by John, Stuart Sutcliffe and their other student cronies in boisterous lunchtime drinking sessions. His romance with fellow art student Cynthia Powell from posh 'over the water' Hoylake on the Wirral also blossomed here.

Frequently, they would be joined by their lecturer and ally, Arthur Ballard, who even conducted tutorials in the back room of the pub. John, who had recently lost his mother in an horrific road accident, drowned his sorrows here and often returned to the Art College in a drunken state. He later admitted: "When I went to art college in Liverpool, you know, it was mainly one long drinking session."

Drinking on one occasion was temporarily abandoned when the then-famous Liverpool-born film star John Gregson appeared outside the pub. Lennon, in typically unconventional fashion, managed to get his autograph...on a dirty old boot that was lying around. On another occasion John pretended to 'swim' in pools of beer on the bar room floor!

A commemorative plaque inside the pub marks the occasion when, in June 1960, four art students (John Lennon, Stuart Sutcliffe, Bill Harry and Rod Murray) attended a poetry reading by Royston Ellis. The four came here to discuss what they had heard. They were unimpressed and decided to put Liverpool on the map, each in his own way as 'The Dissenters'.

(Return to Hope Street and its junction with Mount Street)

FORMER LIVERPOOL INSTITUTE
Mount Street –
PAUL & GEORGE'S HIGH SCHOOL NOW LIVERPOOL INSTITUTE FOR PERFORMING ART (LIPA)

Since 1837 this building had been home to the Liverpool Institute, or the 'Innie' as it was known, and was the city's top high school for boys. It was every Liverpool mother's dream that her son would pass the eleven-plus examination and win one of the prized places here even though he would be branded a 'college pudding' by his lesser talented and no doubt envious mates.

The Innie's two most famous sons were Paul and George. Academically, they were poles apart. Paul had already been here a year when George started in 1954; the Innie was to be their school until they left for Hamburg in 1960. Disinterested and rebellious from the start, George frittered away his opportunities and failed all his exams. He made a mockery of his school uniform by wearing tight drainpipe trousers and, once, a canary yellow waistcoat under his black school blazer. Not for George the regulation 'short back and sides' haircut. He grew his hair as long as he could, piled high in the Elvis and Tony Curtis styles of the day and topped by the universally hated school cap.

April 1956, the Liverpool Institute's Lower School (part 1 - see overleaf for part 2)

Mike McCartney, Paul's younger brother.   *Paul McCartney*

The Liverpool Institute's two most famous 'old boys', George and Paul. Their passion was for rock and roll rather than Latin.

"A boy with little academic ability. Art is the only subject at which he has made any effort." said a school report card, prepared in April 1959 for the Liverpool Youth Employment Bureau. It also noted that he was in the bottom five in his form and that he had expressed a desire to be a 'student fitter'.

Whilst by no means an enthusiastic scholar, Paul was a natural student with the knack of being able to listen to the radio and do his school homework at the same time. He did just enough to get a respectable five GCE 'O' level and one 'A' level passes, failing in History, Geography, Scripture and German.

Neil Aspinall, The Beatles' Road Manager.

Len Garry bass player with the Quarry Men.

Don Andrew and the late Colin Manley, bass player and lead guitarist, respectively, of the Remo Four.

One of his old maths books from Class 4B, filled with doodles and scribbles, fetched £23,000 at a Tokyo auction in 1997.

The Institute had one big plus for Paul and George. It was next door to the Art College, venue for practice sessions with John Lennon and Stu Sutcliffe.

Following its closure in 1985, the Institute was given a new lease of life when Paul announced plans to convert it into a 'School of Fame' or, to give it its full and proper title 'The Liverpool Institute for Performing Arts' – 'LIPA' for short. "The initial reason for my involvement with LIPA was the building. It was my old school. When I saw for myself the state it had reached as an abandoned building, I wanted to save it." From drawing board to official opening took six years, the process being kicked off by a £1 million pound personal donation from Paul. This was followed by the pennies of Liverpool schoolchildren and the millions of pounds of sponsorship ploughed in by Grundig. Even the Queen and celebrities such as Eddie Murphy, Jane Fonda, Ralph Lauren and David Hockney contributed towards the £12 million cost of the venture.

The first 200 hundred students, chosen from applications that flooded in from around the world, started their three-year degree courses in January 1996. Towards the end of that first month, Paul McCartney, watched by Beatles record producer, George Martin, and Chief Executive, Mark Featherstone Witty, officially inaugurated LIPA by cutting a giant cake in the shape of his old school. On the same occasion, Paul's old school assembly hall (now a 450-seat working theatre) was named the Paul McCartney Auditorium. But the real icing on the cake came when the Queen officially opened LIPA in May 1996. And when Paul was knighted he made his acceptance speech here.

April 1956, the Liverpool Institute's Lower School (part 2)

The late Ivan Vaughan, John's boyhood friend and, briefly, base player with the Quarry Men.

(Top) Peter Sissons, BBC Television newsreader. (Below) the late Alan 'Dusty' Durband, Paul's English master and one-time Chairman of the Everyman Theatre.

30

A £7m expansion plan to erect a new building on the corner of Pilgrim Street and Upper Duke Street has been under consideration for a number of years.

Paul continues his very active involvement with LIPA, attending its graduation ceremonies and giving masterclasses to its students.

FORMER LIVERPOOL COLLEGE OF ART
Hope Street. JOHN'S ART COLLEGE

Clutching a portfolio of his work from Quarry Bank High School and wearing his dead Uncle George's sports jacket and a collar and tie specially for the occasion, John scraped through the interview and was accepted as a student here in Summer, 1957.

The college was a big disappointment to the idealistic seventeen year old Lennon. He was immediately strapped into the straightjacket of the lettering class with its overriding requirement for neatness and precision. John loathed it. It was totally alien to his restless, free-roaming spirit.

The only tutor to be on the same wavelength as John was Arthur Ballard who observed: "He draws naturally. As a conventional art student he was not very good but as an artist, which is very much more important, he was very talented."

Cynthia Lennon pictured in 1984 when she opened 'The Art of The Beatles' exhibition at the Walker Art Gallery. Nearly three decades earlier she had found herself in the same art class as the teddy boy teenager John Lennon.

George Harrison

Les Chadwick, bass guitarist with Gerry & the Pacemeakers.

"When I left Quarry Bank I went to the Liverpool College of Art with an idea that I might finish up drawing gorgeous girls for toothpaste photos." John

John's former Art College has been bought by Maghull Developments who plan to convert it into residential apartments.

John himself later said of the three years he spent here: "All I ever learned in art school was about Van Gogh and stuff. They didn't teach me anything about Marcel Duchamp which I despised them for."

It was here that he struck up a close friendship with the very talented Stuart Sutcliffe and met his future wife Cynthia Powell. Polite and twin set prim, she must have appeared an unlikely partner for the disruptive and aggressive 'teddy boy' Lennon with his drainpipe trousers, long drape jacket, sideburns and D.A. (duck's arse) hairstyle.

At an end of term college party, Lennon sounded her out for a date. Awkwardly, Cynthia explained: "I'm awfully sorry, but I'm engaged to this fellow in Hoylake." to which Lennon acidly retorted: "I didn't ask you to marry me did I?" However, she did accept an invitation to join him and his mates for a drink in "Ye Cracke". After the drinking session they went back to Stu Sutcliffe's flat and made love. From then on their infatuation was mutual. They became inseparable. Their relationship was to end in acrimony in 1968 following John's affair with the Japanese artist Yoko Ono. He had first met Yoko in November 1966 at a private preview of her avant-garde art exhibition at London's Indica Gallery.

Sometimes an angel, more often a devil, his years at art college were difficult ones. As John later admitted: "I was in a sort of blind rage for two years. I was either drunk or fighting…There was something the matter with me."

The archetypal 'angry young man' both amused and appalled his fellow students with his grim humour mostly aimed at disabled or old people. "Some people will do anything to get out of the army." he'd shout after cripples. Cruel drawings showed women cooing "Aren't they lovely." over babies with horribly contorted faces. On the day the Pope died a Lennon cartoon showed him locked outside the gates of Heaven with the caption – "But I'm the Pope I tell you!"

In the basement was the college canteen, arched and dimly lit and reminiscent of the Cavern. Here, on the stage at the back, John, Cyn and Stu, joined by Paul and George with fish and chips from the local 'chippy', would gather for practice sessions.

Some of the embryonic Beatles' earliest gigs were played here in the hall during Saturday night college dances. When they set off for Hamburg, they 'borrowed' the college's amplifier!

On a snowy 24 January 1984, Yoko brought Sean on a 'pilgrimage' to Liverpool to see some of his father's old haunts. They called here and generously presented the college with a complete set of John's Bag One lithographs. Rather embarrassingly, the valuable gift was later stolen from the college library. Their trip echoed an earlier pilgrimage Yoko and John had made to Liverpool in 1970. It was to be his last visit to the city.

(Right) John posed for fellow student, Ann Mason, in this unique and unusual portrait. Unusual? Short-sighted and vain, John hated to be seen wearing his spectacles.

(At the next junction, turn left into Canning Street then right into Percy Street.)

N0.9 PERCY STREET
STU SUTCLIFFE'S FLAT

Here in the rear of the first floor of No 9 was the one-room 'flat' occupied by John's art college friends, Stu Sutcliffe, The Beatles' first bass player, often referred to as 'The Fifth Beatle', and Rod Murray. With his James Dean-like persona, Stu epitomised the romantic image of 'the sensitive artist'. He was regarded as 'brilliant' by his tutor Arthur Ballard, who gave him personal tuition here.

(Return to the junction of Canning Street and Hope Street. Here there is a gated entrance to Gambier Terrace.)

3 GAMBIER TERRACE –
JOHN'S FLAT

Much against his Aunt Mimi's advice, John left the comforts of 'Mendips' to share a flat here in 1960 with Stu Sutcliffe and Rod Murray, another student from art college. It was also a good place to spend time with Cynthia. Many was the night she spent here with John having hoodwinked her mother into believing she was staying over with a girlfriend.

The flat was an ideal place for John and Stu to draw and paint together and for The Beatles to rehearse; soon they would be off to Hamburg.

When John and Stu set off for Hamburg from here with the rest of the Beatles in Summer 1960, John left all his possessions in Rod Murray's flat. A year later he suggested to Rod that he should keep anything he wanted and throw the rest away. He kept only two items and in 1984 at Sotheby's Rock and Roll Memorabilia auction in London he sold one of John's school exercise books containing 16 pages of poetry, prose, drawings and cartoons for £16,000. The value, in both artistic and monetary terms, of the material thrown away by Rod does not bear thinking about.

According to Paul, it was here in Gambier Terrace that John and Stu announced that they wanted to call the band 'The Beatles'.

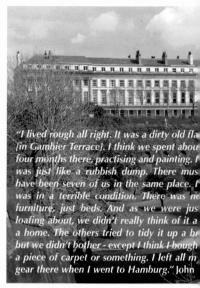

"I lived rough all right. It was a dirty old fla [in Gambier Terrace]. I think we spent abou four months there, practising and painting. I was just like a rubbish dump. There mus have been seven of us in the same place. I was in a terrible condition. There was no furniture, just beds. And as we were jus loafing about, we didn't really think of it a a home. The others tried to tidy it up a br but we didn't bother - except I think I bough a piece of carpet or something. I left all m gear there when I went to Hamburg." John

(The apartments in Gambier Terrace have splendid views of what is, by reason of its sheer size, Liverpool's most prominent building, the Anglican Cathedral. The entrance can be found down the hill near the junction of Upper Duke Street and Rodney Street.)

LIVERPOOL CATHEDRAL *Upper Duke Street*

This monumental building is the city's Anglican Cathedral. It was here that a Beatle was rejected because his singing voice was not thought good enough! In 1953 Paul McCartney auditioned here for a place in the cathedral choir but was unsuccessful. In a delicious touch of irony he returned in June 1991 for the world premiere of the partly autobiographical *Liverpool Oratorio,* the symphony he wrote in collaboration with Carl Davis to celebrate the 150th anniversary of the Royal Liverpool Philharmonic Orchestra.

It's an awe-inspiring building, the biggest cathedral in Britain and, after St John the Divine in New York, the largest Anglican cathedral in the world. On Sunday 29th March 1981 it became the fitting venue for a special memorial service when the people of Liverpool paid their official last respects to John Lennon. During this moving 'Festival of Peace' a selection of Lennon and McCartney songs was played on the cathedral's mighty 9765-pipe organ.

There are spectacular views over the city from atop the 331ft tower and good food is served in the Refectory. It's an awesome building and a visit is a 'must'.

(Continue down the hill to the traffic lights. Note the spectacular Chinese arch, the biggest in the world outside mainland China, and a symbol of Liverpool's Chinatown, the oldest in Europe. Straight ahead is Duke Street. Number 139 was once 'Joe's Cafe', a late night eating and meeting place during the Merseybeat era for The Beatles and other musicians. The owner, Joe Davey, subsequently became the owner of the Cavern during its declining years. Near the bottom of the street, at number 28, was the Cabaret Club which passed for sophistication in the Liverpool of the early 60's. Although they socialised here, The Beatles only played here once, on 25th July 1962, to an unappreciative audience. Cross to the right into Berry Street and continue along to Seel Street, on the opposite side of the road. Near the top of Seel Street, on the left hand side, is the Blue Angel club.)

BLUE ANGEL CLUB *108 Seel Street*

Previously called the Wyvern Social Club, this was the setting for two legendary auditions. In 1960, London rock impresario Larry Parnes was looking for a band to back his star protégé Billy Fury. The Silver Beetles, with 'borrowed' drummer Johnny Hutchinson of Cass and the Cassanovas (later the Big Three), didn't pass the audition held on 10th May in the dingy basement...Stu's bass playing was less than adequate. But they obviously impressed Parnes. He later hired them for a tour of Scotland with one of his other stars, fellow Liverpudlian Johnny Gentle.

Billy Fury was Liverpool's first rock and roll star and had been appearing in the UK charts since the beginning of 1959. Small wonder that a star-struck John Lennon had asked Billy for his autograph. Also watching the five groups being auditioned that day was Rory Storm, leader of Rory Storm and the Hurricanes...whose drummer was Ringo Starr.

Pete Best was drummer with his Casbah-based group the Blackjacks when Paul telephoned that Summer to invite him to join The Beatles for their first trip to Hamburg. But first he had to audition here on 12th August 1960 prior to joining John, Paul, George and Stu as 'the Fifth Beatle'. Four days later they all set off for Hamburg.

The following year, now as the Blue Angel, the club was being run by The Beatles' 'manager' Allan Williams. The 'Blue' became *the* place for Liverpool musicians including The Beatles, although for a time Williams banned them from the club for non-payment of his manager's commission. It was also the natural choice for other stars visiting Liverpool. In those days you could have rubbed shoulders with the Rolling Stones, Bob Dylan, Judy Garland and, before she became famous, Cilla Black.

(Continue along Berry Street to the next set of traffic lights at the junction of Bold Street and Renshaw Street.)

81a RENSHAW STREET – FORMER OFFICE OF 'MERSEY BEAT'

The *Mersey Beat* newspaper was an avidly read guide to the local music scene produced by Bill Harry, an art college friend of John and Stu.

The second page of the first edition, published on 6th July 1961, featured a typically Lennonesque article under the headline – 'Being a Short Diversion on the Dubious Origins of Beatles'. He explained how The Beatles came by their name...It came in a vision – a man

Bill Harry pictured in the reconstruction of the Mersey Beat office in The Beatles Story, Albert Dock.

appeared on a flaming pie and said unto them "From this day on you are Beatles with an A." *Flaming Pie* was also the title Paul gave to his 1997 album.

Until its demise some 90 editions later Bill's beat scene 'bible' recorded The Beatles' rise to fame. Frequent callers and regular contributors to *Mersey Beat*, which had its offices here above a wine merchant's shop next door to the Roscoe Arms pub, included The Beatles and Brian Epstein who reviewed records for the paper. During a Mersey Beat office move, a large bundle of John's stories and poems, written for the paper under his 'Beatcomber' pseudonym, managed to get 'lost'.

Another regular caller was Cavern DJ Bob Wooler who wrote a column called 'The Roving I'. The first article ever written about The Beatles was one penned by Bob for Mersey Beat in mid-1961. Needless to say, copies of *Mersey Beat* are now much sought after collector's items.

Bill Harry is an authority on The Beatles. A prolific writer, he is the author of a score of books about them including *The Book of Lennon*, *The Beatles Who's Who*, and *The Beatles Encyclopedia*. Find out more on Bill's excellent website: *www.mersey-beat.net*

(Turn left into Bold Street.)

BOLD STREET (1)

On the right hand side, at number 89, near the top of the street, was the Odd Spot Club, venue for two Beatles gigs during 1962. John Dykins, partner of John's mother, Julia, was once a waiter here.

At No 83, was Kaye Photography. When Brian Epstein needed new publicity photographs of The Beatles with the just-recruited Ringo he turned to one of Liverpool's best-known social photographers, Bill Connell, alias Peter Kaye. In those days Bill had a shop in Park Road and a modest studio in Newington, a rather shabby side street off Bold Street. Later he moved his operations to Bold Street, known in its heyday as 'The Bond Street of the North'. Those early historic images of The Beatles taken by Bill and his young assistant Les Chadwick in their studio, on derelict sites in Liverpool's docklands (opposite page, bottom), in the Cavern and other Mersey Beat-era venues can be seen in Peter Kaye's *Beatles in Liverpool*, largely put together by Bill's assistant, Margaret Roberts, and published in 1987. Sadly, Bill, a flamboyant, larger-than-life character, died the following year and Apple now owns the copyright of most of his photographs. See also next page for another Bold Street Beatle landmark.

(Continue down Bold Street and turn left into Slater Street. Near its junction with Seel Street, is the Jacaranda Club. Also notice the Marlborough pub, another occasional watering hole during The Beatles' early years.)

JACARANDA CLUB *23 Slater Street*

Once owned by Allan Williams, the 'Jac' was a favourite place for The Beatles to hang out during their student days in the late 1950's. They would sit in the window playing their guitars, munching the Jac's famous bacon butties and making sarcastic remarks to the office girls coming in for a lunchtime snack. Downstairs, in the evening, the tiny airless basement reverberated to the then unlikely sound of the immensely popular 'Royal Caribbean' West Indian steel band. I can personally vouch that it was like the Black Hole of Calcutta, far sweatier than the Cavern!

The Beatles played about a dozen lunchtime and Monday evening engagements from May 1960 when the Royal Caribbean had their night off. Their payment? Coca Cola and beans on toast!

Allan Williams presents a Beatles fan with a copy of his book 'Allan Williams as The Fool On The Hill...how the beat went on after his BIG BEATLES blunder'.

Also picture the scene on Tuesday, 15th August 1960 as the five Beatles, Allan Williams, his wife Beryl and her brother Barry Chang, and Allan's Caribbean friend 'Lord Woodbine', all crammed into Allan's battered old van and set off on their eventful journey to Hamburg.

The completely refurbished Jac reopened in 1996 with Pete and his Pete Best Band on stage. Pete commented – "It was in the Jacaranda that I first appeared with The Beatles, just before they went over to Germany – it would have been way back in August 1960. We were so poor in those days, we had our girlfriends sitting in the front with mike stands strapped to broom handles. But it was excellent. It was the place to be; everyone used to arrange to meet up at the Jac."

Basement murals, supposedly painted by John and Stu Sutcliffe during their art student days, were restored in time for the re-opening.

However, the original Jacaranda Club looked very different from the present one; it occupied only half the frontage of the present club, the half adjacent to the Marlborough pub, another occasional haunt of the early Beatles.

(Retrace your steps to Bold Street and turn left.)

Liverpool City Centre

BOLD STREET (2)

At the bottom of Bold Street is the old Lyceum building which once housed Reece's 'Lyceum Cafe', an old-fashioned Liverpool institution now sadly gone. Nowadays it houses a branch of the Co-operative Bank. The Beatles used to meet here for coffee and, it is said, pass the time composing songs on the backs of menus and table napkins.

(At the bottom of Bold Street, look left to the building next to the bank)

In its Victorian heyday, Bold Street was dubbed 'The Bond Street of the north'. One contemporary observer noted: "In this street can be seen the toffs of Liverpool". The Lyceum (left) was built in 1803 to house England's first 'gentleman's subscription library'.

EPSTEIN THEATRE (*formerly Neptune Theatre*) Hanover Street

In August 1997, on the 30th anniversary of Brian Epstein's death, Liverpool City Council dedicated their theatre to his memory. Paul remarked – "Brian would have loved this, to have a theatre in his name. He was always very keen on acting." Actually, Brian once did buy a theatre of his very own…the *Saville* in London's Shaftesbury Avenue in April 1965. The theatre 'sat' on top of Crane's music store which, along with Rushworth's and Hessy's, were the three most frequented by Merseybeat-era musicians.

(Cross at the traffic lights into pedestrianised Church Street. The next street on the right is Parker Street.)

FORMER REECE'S RESTAURANT
Above Superdrug store, Parker Street/Leigh Street

Reece's first floor restaurant was the unlikely venue for John and Cynthia's wedding breakfast on 23rd August 1962. After their wedding in the Mount Pleasant Registry Office, they dashed through the pouring rain with Paul, George and Brian in tow to fight for a table along with dozens of other lunchtime shoppers and office workers. The set lunch of soup, roast chicken and trifle was paid for by Brian. The newly-weds were toasted with water since the restaurant was not licensed to serve alcohol during the daytime.

(Continue along Church Street to School Lane, on the left. Facing you at the end of School Lane is Bluecoat Chambers.)

BLUECOAT CHAMBERS
School Lane

Dating from 1717, this stunning Queen Anne period building, the oldest in Liverpool city centre, is the legacy of a Liverpool slave trader and do-gooder, Bryan Blundell...the city has always been a place of contradiction and controversy!

Long a centre for the arts, Yoko Ono (pictured below) appeared here on 26th September 1967 in a 'happening', a phenomenon of the 60's that seemed even dafter then than it would do now. People sat dangling their legs over the stage eating sandwiches. The audience was invited to come on stage to chalk messages on a blackboard. And, as a climax, Yoko (below) was bound to a chair with bandages and enveloped in smoke!

Less than a year earlier John had met Yoko for the first time at a private viewing of her avant-garde exhibition at London's Indica Gallery. Although he didn't know it at the time, he had met his soul mate.

In 1990 the Bluecoat staged an exhibition of works by Stuart Sutcliffe.

Following a radical £12.5m transformation, the complex reopened in March 2008 in time to celebrate the city's year as European Capital of Culture.

(Continue along Church Street to its junction with Paradise Street and Whitechapel. McDonald's has replaced Horne Brothers the gentlemen's outfitters in the basement of which was a barber shop where Brian Epstein sent The Beatles as part of his smarten up plan. Opposite, in Lord Street, was Times Furnishing where Brian served a six month sales apprenticeship for a weekly wage of £5 when he was 18 years old. Turn right into Whitechapel.)

...s part of the Bluecoat's re-pening programme, Yoko Ono staged an exclusive live performance on 4th April.

Get your 'BEAT' and 'Rhythm & Blues'
Records at . . .

NEMS

Whitechapel & Gt. Charlotte St.
Largest Selection of Popular Records in the North

FORMER NEMS RECORD SHOP & HQ
12 Whitechapel (near junction with Church St.)

Legend has it that, on 28th October 1961, a youth called Raymond Jones walked into NEMS record store and asked, without success, for *My Bonnie* by The Beatles. He had heard the record, a scorching rocker, at Hambleton Hall also known as the 'Hive of Jive', played by promoter/DJ Bob Wooler.

Wooler had encouraged his youthful audience to ask for it at their record shops. Local teenager Raymond Jones took his advice and asked Brian Epstein for the record at this store. Epstein prided himself on being able to search out any record asked for by his customers and tracked down the elusive record which turned out to be a minor best seller for him. Curious to find out more about the group that

The NEMS building, an important site on the Beatles heritage trail, was demolished in February 2012 to make way for a new store.

he claimed he'd never heard of before, he decided to visit the nearby Cavern club on 9 November 1961 when The Beatles were making one of their regular lunch-time appearances. The rest, as they say, is history.

It has since been suggested that Epstein was fully aware of The Beatles' popularity months before Raymond Jones asked him for their record. Surely, it is argued, the astute Epstein could not have avoided seeing the prominent coverage given to them on the front covers of *Mersey Beat*, the newspaper for which he both wrote reviews and sold in his store, or the dance tickets sold by NEMS which bore The Beatles' name.

THE BEATLES
FIRST RECORD ON PARLOPHONE
LOVE ME DO
c/w
P.S. I LOVE YOU
RELEASED FRIDAY OCTOBER 5th
12-14, WHITECHAPEL. Tel. ROYal. 7895
50, GREAT CHARLOTTE ST. 70-72, WALTON RD.
NEMS

The upstairs office here soon became the nerve centre for Brian's burgeoning NEMS Enterprises of which The Beatles were central.

By the Summer of 1963 the meteoric growth of NEMS Enterprises had led to the office being re-located from here to first floor premises above the Wizard's Den joke shop at 24 Moorfields, a few streets away. In March of the following year Brian moved the entire NEMS Enterprises operation to London.

Liverpool City Centre

FORMER RUSHWORTH'S MUSIC HOUSE
Corner of Whitechapel/Richmond Street

Rushworth's was Liverpool's largest musical instrument suppliers and something of a Liverpool institution. Many of the Merseybeat groups, including The Beatles, bought their gear here. Their much-prized Gibson acoustic-electric guitars were specially flown in from Chicago and formally presented to them by James Rushworth the firm's Chairman (pictured below). John always lamented that his favourite Gibson had somehow gone 'missing' on one of their later tours.

Paul's dad bought him a trumpet from Rushworths for his birthday. Realising that he couldn't sing with a trumpet stuck in his mouth he soon swapped it for a Zenith acoustic guitar. Paul still has it in his guitar collection.

Sadly, the 170 year old business, which in its heyday billed itself as the: 'Five Generation Music House - the largest in Europe', folded in 2000 and the building is now home to a number of small businesses.

(Turn left into Stanley Street.)

Liverpool City Centre

FORMER HESSY'S *(Now Wongs Jewellers) Stanley Street*

One of Liverpool's three major musical instrument stores during the Merseybeat years presided over by the ever-present Frank Hessy and his star salesman Jim Gretty. The price of buying a guitar included a three-chord 'lesson' from Jim, a club performer himself. It was Jim who had sold John his first 'proper' £15 guitar in 1957.

One early act of Brian Epstein as their manager was to clear the £200 debt which The Beatles owed Hessy's for John's Hofner Club 40 guitar, George's Futurama guitar and Paul's amplification equipment.

Hessy's later featured in the film *Ferry 'cross the Mersey*.

On the corner of the street, next door to Hessy's, which closed its doors for the last time in 1995, was the Kardomah Coffee House (now also part of Wongs) another Liverpool institution and non-alcoholic hangout for The Beatles.

(Continue up Stanley Street and cross the road to the Eleanor Rigby statue)

41

THE CAVERN QUARTER:

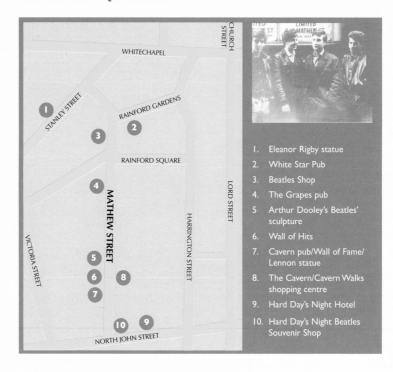

WHITECHAPEL

CHURCH STREET

STANLEY STREET

RAINFORD GARDENS

RAINFORD SQUARE

MATHEW STREET

LORD STREET

HARRINGTON STREET

VICTORIA STREET

NORTH JOHN STREET

1. Eleanor Rigby statue
2. White Star Pub
3. Beatles Shop
4. The Grapes pub
5. Arthur Dooley's Beatles' sculpture
6. Wall of Hits
7. Cavern pub/Wall of Fame/ Lennon statue
8. The Cavern/Cavern Walks shopping centre
9. Hard Day's Night Hotel
10. Hard Day's Night Beatles Souvenir Shop

1) ELEANOR RIGBY STATUE *Stanley Street*

Dedicated to 'all the lonely people'...the mythical, sad figure in the Beatles' famous song, was sculpted by Tommy *'I've never felt more like singing the blues'* Steele as a tribute to the Liverpudlian pop idols.

In the certain knowledge that the City Fathers would not put their hands in their pockets for any memorial to The Beatles, Tommy gave it to them for half a sixpence, just over one penny. The £4,000 which it cost to cast the statue in bronze was met by the Liverpool Echo newspaper.

Almost as interesting as the statue itself is what Tommy enigmatically placed inside it: a four leaf clover for luck, a page from the Bible for spiritual help, a sonnet for lovers, an adventure book for excitement and a pair of football boots for action.

On 3 December 1982 the perky Cockney performed the official unveiling of his creation, explaining – "I put them all inside the statue so she would be full of magical properties. I give Eleanor to Liverpool with an open heart and many thanks for my happy times in the City". Tommy had another date with Eleanor in 2003 when he celebrated her 21st anniversary (*opposite page, top left*).

Opposite the sculpture is the Eleanor Rigby Hotel.

(Retrace your steps and turn right into Mathew Street.)

MATHEW STREET

The Mathew Street you see today is nothing like the narrow, grubby little warehouse street of the Merseybeat era. Nowadays it is part of the trendy 'Cavern Quarter' pub and club scene and has well and truly cashed in on its Beatles heritage. Apart from the Cavern club and Cavern Walks complex, you will find a John Lennon Bar, Rubber Soul pub, and the Beatles souvenir shops. Even the humble electricity sub-station has had a make-over. There is also is a Cavern Pub which has one of the Hofner bass guitars made famous by Paul. "Cool Cavern! Cheers! Paul McCartney Dec 14 '99" he wrote on the scratchplate.

(Look down Rainford Gardens and you will see The White Star pub.)

2) WHITE STAR PUB *Rainford Gardens*

Mecca for drinkers of Draft Bass, the White Star was an alternative venue to the Grapes pub for The Beatles and the other groups appearing at the Cavern.

3) THE BEATLES SHOP

Above the doorway is a sculpture by local artist David Hughes, the city's first Beatles sculpture and still the only one in Liverpool which looks remotely like The Beatles. The City's latest ones, full length statues of the Fab Four perched above the polished granite columns of the Hard Days Night Hotel, are laughable, arguably the worst so far, and spoil the elegant facade of this classical building.

Visitors to the shop have included Sean Lennon, Beatles producer George Martin, Neil Aspinall, head of Apple...and Ringo who popped in to use their telephone!

(Continue walking up Mathew Street)

4) THE GRAPES PUB

'The Beatles' Pub', as it is known, is opposite the Cavern and therefore the obvious choice for the Beatles and other Merseybeat groups. It was a popular refuge from the Cavern where coffee or Coca Cola were the strongest drinks on offer. Here The Beatles would down pints of Brown Mix or Black Velvet and Brian, when he did join them, decorously sipped brandy. When Pete Best was sacked from the Beatles on 16th August 1962, he drowned his sorrows here with their Road Manager, Neil Aspinall.

5) ARTHUR DOOLEY'S BEATLE SCULPTURE

You'll either love or loathe this celebration of the Fab Four by local sculptor the late Arthur Dooley, a giant of a man with a larger-than-life character to match. When it was erected in 1974, this curious dedication to the 'Four Lads Who Shook The World' consisted of four cherubic images fashioned from plastic dolls. A guitar-carrying cherub complete with a 'Lennon Lives' halo was added in 1980.

6) WALL OF HITS

The 'Wall of Hits' is a excellent commemoration of the 56 (as at the end of 2005) No.1. hit records by Liverpool bands and artistes. They range from Lita Roza's 1953 hit *How Much is that Doggie in the Window?* to Atomic Kitten's The *Tide is High* and, of course, includes the 17 Beatles hits and 8 No 1s by individual Beatles/Wings. The wall was unveiled on 14th March, 2001, by the 75 year-old, but still sprightly, Lita Roza.

7) CAVERN PUB/WALL OF FAME/LENNON STATUE

The 40th anniversary of the Cavern was celebrated in style on 16th January 1997. A *Wall of Fame* formed of bricks etched with the names of the 1,801 bands who played the club between 1957 and 1973 was unveiled by Gerry Marsden of Gerry and the Pacemakers. Billy J Kramer unveiled a statue which bears but a passing resemblance to John Lennon. The Cavern Pub opened in 1994 and is themed around the famous bands and stars who played at the Cavern including The Rolling Stones, The Who, Chuck Berry, Jimi Hendrix and, of course, The Beatles.

8) THE CAVERN/CAVERN WALKS

The stylish Cavern Walks complex opened in Spring 1984 and replaced a row of grimy old warehouses. In one of these, number ten, formerly a wine and spirit store, egg packing station and even a make-shift air raid shelter against Hitler's Luftwaffe, 18 stone steps led down to a cellar club the name of which was to become known the world over. That club was the Cavern.

Here, in the catacombed darkness beneath your feet, The Beatles played no less than 274 times. They made their debut

"I loved the Cavern. It was a claustrophobic hell, but it was a great one..." Paul

during the lunchtime of Thursday, 9th February 1961 for £5 and went on to play a further 151 lunch-time sessions. Their final performance, for £300, took place on the evening of Saturday 3rd August 1963. Along with other top local groups, for the Mersey Sound was never just The Beatles, they made the Cavern the most famous rock and roll venue of its day.

But the Cavern had not always echoed to the big beat sound. When doctor's son Alan Sytner bought it in 1956 he planned a similar venture to 'Le Caveau Francais', the Parisian jazz club. The Cavern first opened its doors to a jazz-only crowd on 16th January 1957, but soon yielded to the skiffle craze sweeping the country at that time. It was to be the thin end of a very large rock and roll wedge.

Indeed, it was as the Quarry Men skiffle group that the young Beatles made their first true appearance at the Cavern on Wednesday, 7th August 1957. Paul missed this historic event. He was away at a Boy Scout Summer camp at the time. And six months were to pass before the 14 year old George Harrison was to meet the Quarry Men for the first time. The original 1957 Quarry Men line-up (minus John Lennon and of course it wasn't the *real* Cavern) played their first gig at the Cavern almost 42 years to the day of their debut appearance.

Maggie May, Railroad Bill, Cumberland Gap and other Lonnie Donegan skiffle numbers would have been been as much a part of the Beatles' repertoire in those days as their distinctive versions of Elvis, Chuck Berry and Buddy Holly classics. More significantly, by this time, the first hesitant efforts of the Lennon/McCartney song-writing partnership were also being given an airing.

the CAVERN

PRESENTS ITS EVENING SESSIONS
7–12 p.m.

SATURDAY, 9th JUNE

THE BEATLES

FIRST APPEARANCE FOLLOWING THEIR
SUCCESS IN GERMANY

THE RED RIVER JAZZMEN
KEN DALLAS AND THE
SILHOUETTES
THE FOUR JAYS

Don't you rock me Daddy-O

In 1959 the Cavern passed into the hands of accountant Ray McFall. Although rock and roll had occasionally sneaked in, much to the disgust of the regular jazz purists, it was not until 25th May 1960 that McFall relented to allow the very first beat night. On stage that night were the immensely popular Cass and the Cassanovas (later the Big Three) and Rory Storm and the Hurricanes whose drummer was none other than Ringo Starr. From that night the Cavern was 'lost' to rock and roll.

Welcoming fans to 'the best of cellars', the Cavern's legendary DJ, Bob Wooler, the 'Prince of Pun', introduced the cream of the hundreds of Merseyside groups that had emerged out of the short-lived skiffle boom – the Searchers, the Swinging Blue Jeans, the Remo Four, Gerry and the Pacemakers, Billy J Kramer and the Dakotas, the Fourmost, the Big Three and, of course, The Beatles. And there was a girl singer, the Cavern's cloakroom attendant Priscilla White, better known as Cilla Black.

'Legends in their own lunchtime'

On Thursday, 9th November 1961, during one of its famous lunchtime sessions, a sober-suited 27 year old Brian Epstein visited the Cavern to see for himself its star performers, The Beatles. He watched. He listened. He was hooked. Despite the warnings of Allan Williams, their first manager, "not to touch them with a f***ing barge-pole", Brian eventually signed them up in his NEMS office in nearby Whitechapel on Wednesday 24th January 1962.

To say that The Beatles' stage persona at the time of Brian's first visit was 'informal' would be a gross under-statement. They would smoke cigarettes, drink tea and eat jam butties on stage, crack jokes, swear, and exchange banter with the audience. Brian would soon change all that.

Cavern of Dreams

Amid howls of protest, the debt-ridden Cavern was closed down by the Official Receiver on 28th February 1966. It was ceremoniously re-opened five months later on 23rd July by Prime Minister Harold Wilson who was presented with a wooden pipe crafted from the original stage which had been broken up in 1964 and sold piece by piece for charity.

Although it survived for another seven years, it closed its doors for the last time on 27th May 1973 as Paul McCartney and his new group Wings played the final night of their UK tour at the Hammersmith Odeon Cinema. The warehouse was then bulldozed to provide a working site for the construction of the city's new underground railway system. Most Beatle fans remain amazed that the City of Liverpool did nothing to stop this act of cultural vandalism. And who can blame them?

For a number of years the historic Cavern site was an unsightly temporary car park before it was bought by the Liverpool-based company Royal Life (now Resolution) and redeveloped into the Cavern Walks shops and office complex that you see today.

The Cavern Lives!

Cavern Walks bristles with Beatle features. Cynthia Lennon designed the terra-cotta embellishments to its frontage. In the shopping mall look out for the 'official' statue to

the Fab Four by John Doubleday (right), unveiled by Mike McCartney who, non-plussed, quizzed... "Which one's our kid?!"

Most exciting of all, the Cavern club was rebuilt as near to the original as possible using bricks saved from the old Cavern. Whilst it is not an exact replica and can never recapture the magical atmosphere of the original Cavern, it is worth a visit since it's the nearest thing to the real Cavern that you can experience. Another, smaller scale, replica can be found in The Beatles Story at Albert Dock.

The high spot for the 'new' Cavern came on 14th December 1999 when Paul performed his last gig of the millennium here in front of 150 lucky fans and a similar number of media people. Paul explained - "I am going back for just one night as a nod to the music that has and will ever thrill me. I can't think of a better way to rock out the end of the century than with a rock 'n' roll gig at the Cavern."

To the right of the main entrance door of 8 Mathew Street is a display (pictured right) marking the site of the entrance door to the original Cavern club.

Mathew Street is a focal point for the *Mathew Street Festival* which takes place every August. It embraces venues throughout the city centre and attracts tens of thousands of people including many from overseas.

10) HARD DAYS NIGHT HOTEL
Central Buildings, North John Street

Whilst a Beatles-themed hotel in Liverpool had been under discussion for many years, it was only on 1st February 2008 that The Hard Days Night Hotel finally opened. This fab four-star 'boutique' hotel is ideally located in a beautiful restored Grade Two Listed building dating from 1884 on the corner of Mathew Street and North John Street, just yards away from the famous Cavern club, spiritual home of the Fab Four.

Each of the 110 bedrooms, and two penthouses – the Lennon and McCartney suites – is adorned with specially-commissioned artwork by internationally acclaimed American airbrush artist Shannon.

The public areas of the hotel include Blakes restaurant, Bar Four, the Live Lounge and The Lounge & Bar. There are also conference rooms for private entertaining and corporate events – Beatles fans can even get married in the unique Wedding Suite! On the Mathew Street corner of the hotel is a very well stocked Beatles souvenir shop.

Information: www.harddaysnighthotel.com ● Bookings: +44 (0)151 236 1964

"As a kid I used to go to their garden parties with my friends Ivan, Nigel and Pete. We'd all go up there and hang out and sell lemonade bottles. We always had fun at Strawberry Field." John

SOUTH LIVERPOOL

1. 9 Madryn Street
2. 10 Admiral Grove
3. Empress Pub
4. St Silas School
5. Dingle Vale School
6. 37 Aigburth Drive
7. Sefton General
8. 93 Garmoyle Road
9. Penny Lane
10. St Barnabas Hall
11. Dovedale Rd School
12. 9 Newcastle Road
13. Mosspits Lne School
14. 12 Arnold Grove
15. 197 Queens Drive
16. Quarry Bank School
17. Strawberry Field
18. 251 Menlove Avenue
19. St Peter's Church
20. 174 Mackets Lane
21. 20 Forthlin Road
22. 1 Blomfield Road
23. Allerton Cemetery
24. Wilson Hall
25. 72 Western Avenue
26. Stockton Wd School
27. 25 Upton Green
28. 12 Ardwick Road

Magical History Tour

Here is a selection of some of the more important Beatle places outside the city centre but still within or near the Liverpool boundary. For ease, I've grouped them under South Liverpool and North & East Liverpool.

The number after each of the addresses indicates the postal districts into which the city is divided. However, to help you find your way around the city, I suggest you buy a good street map, available from most bookshops, many newsagents or local Tourist Information Centres.

All the places can be reached by public transport; for information, 'phone the Merseytravel Line on 0151 236 7676 seven days a week 8am to 8pm or visit the Queen Square Travel Centre (www.merseytravel.gov.uk).

'RINGOLAND' – The Dingle

NO 9 MADRYN STREET *off High Park Street, Dingle, Liverpool 8*
RINGO'S BIRTHPLACE

Humble birthplace of the eldest Beatle. Richard ('Richy') Starkey, alias Ringo Starr, was born in the front room of this Victorian terraced house on 7th July 1940, a month before Hitler started his bombing raids on the nearby docks.

Ringo was just three when his mother Elsie and father, also Richard, split up. Elsie worked as a part-time barmaid to make ends meet, leaving young Ringo either with neighbours or more often than not with Grandma and Grandad Starkey who lived at the very end of the street at No 59 (pictured below right). Grandad Starkey, a boilerman who worked at the docks, once made

"Ringo was the only real city kid... I think he came out of the lousiest area. He doesn't care, he probably had more fun there." John

South Liverpool

Ringo a big train 'with a real fire in the engine' which not surprisingly was the talk of the street. Fitting then that much later in life Ringo should be so closely associated with the popular 'Thomas the Tank Engine' stories for which he did the voice-over.

February 2012 – Ringo's birthplace, his grandparents' house (extreme right), and every other house in this Madryn Street terrace, is boarded up and awaits its fate – regeneration or the wrecking ball?

Partly because the rent was cheaper, partly to avoid bumping into her ex-husband who was also living in Madryn Street, but mainly to help an old friend who had a husband and three children, Elsie swapped her house for her friend's even smaller 'two up, two down' house in nearby Admiral Grove when Ringo was six years old.

After many years of dereliction and abandonment, Ringo's birthplace was sold at a Tokyo auction in March 1997 for £13,250 and subsequently renovated. However, in September 2005, Liverpool City Council decided that Madryn Street along with ten other neighbouring Victorian streets should be bulldozed. In a partial reprieve, the City Council perversely pledged that, although Ringo's birthplace had no historical significance, it would be dismantled brick by brick and stored safely away until it could finally be decided where it could be re-built. Disappointingly, a plan to re-built it in the new Museum of Liverpool under construction at the Pier Head was abandoned. Nowadays, Ringo divides his time between homes in Los Angeles, Monte Carlo and Surrey, England, although he did find time to petition for these homes to be saved and renovated.

"Our neighbourhood was really bombe[d] We had to hide a lot, I've been told sin[ce] we used to hide in the coal cellar (it was l[ike] a cupboard). I remember big gaps in t[he] streets where houses stood. We used to p[lay] on the rubble when I was older, and in t[he] air-raid shelters." Ringo

NO.10 ADMIRAL GROVE
off High Park Street, Liverpool 8
RINGO'S HOUSE

Ringo's tiny 'two up, two down' home from the age of six until fame and fortune beyond his wildest imaginings were heaped on his humble shoulders after just six months as the Beatles' new drummer. Ever since, it seems to me, Ringo has had that permanent "How did all these wonderful things happen to an 'ordinary' little boy from Liverpool like me?" look about him!

Ringo's mother re-married in April 1954 when he was nearly 14. Her new husband, whom she had known for many years, was a Londoner called Harry Graves. After the war and an illness, he had come to Liverpool to take up a place on a Government training scheme for painters and decorators and, amazingly, 'for a beneficial change of air'! Remember, in those pre-Clean Air Act days, Liverpool had a well-deserved reputation for being one of the most air-polluted and soot-blackened cities in Britain, a place where lung-searing smogs were common.

The irony was compounded that same year when Ringo caught a cold which developed into pleurisy and affected his lungs. He was sent to convalesce at the Children's Hospital at Heswall on the healthy Wirral coast. He remained there for six months...but he was the drummer in the ward band!

52

To Elsie's joy, Ringo and Harry hit it off from the start. Unwittingly, it was Harry who probably sparked off Ringo's fascination for all things American including a thwarted teenage attempt to emigrate to Texas. Harry was a painter at the giant United States Air Force base at Burtonwood near Liverpool and he often brought home the genuine American 'DC' comics, film magazines, candy and gum much prized by Liverpool children who usually had to make do with inferior English substitutes. He was also a very good singer and the 'star turn' at family parties.

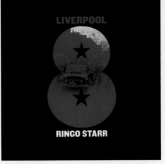

Ringo sings about Madryn Street and Admiral Grove on his 'Liverpool 8' album.

When he left school at 15 having missed so much of his education through illness, Ringo became, in rapid succession, a British Rail messenger boy, a steward on the cruise boat *St. Tudno* that once sailed between Liverpool and Llandudno and an apprentice fitter with local firm, H. Hunt and Son. Also at Hunts was his next door neighbour Ed Miles. During the skiffle craze Ringo joined his Eddie Clayton Skiffle Group.

When he was 20, and by then drummer with the hugely popular Merseybeat group Rory Storm and the Hurricanes, Ringo packed in his apprenticeship at Hunt's and set off with the band to enter the 'big time'… a 13 week season at Butlins Holiday Camp in Pwllheli, North Wales! It was here that he first became known as Ringo Starr and even had his own 'Starr-Time' solo spot with the group.

The following Summer, Ringo celebrated his 21st birthday with a party at 10 Admiral Grove. Difficult though it is to believe, about 60 people crammed into this tiny house, including Cilla Black, Gerry and the Pacemakers and the Big Three.

On 30th August 1963 all four Beatles were here for the filming of footage for the documentary 'The Mersey Sound'. John and Paul took a back seat on this occasion whilst Ringo was filmed emerging through the front door, fighting his way past hordes of small kids and getting into George's open-top car.

Elsie and Harry clung onto their home in the Dingle until 1965 when fan fever became just too much. However, unlike the other Beatle parents, they insisted on staying in Liverpool so Ringo bought them a luxurious bungalow in Woolton, a select area of the city, where they spent their remaining years.

THE EMPRESS PUBLIC HOUSE
High Park Street/Admiral St., Liverpool 8

To Beatle fans who own Ringo's first solo album *Sentimental Journey*, this typical Liverpool street corner pub will look familiar. He used a photograph of it on the front cover; the people in the windows are members of his family. The back cover features the former grocer's shop on the corner of Kinmel Street (opposite The Empress pub).

ST. SILAS CHURCH OF ENGLAND PRIMARY SCHOOL
High Park Street, Liverpool 8
RINGO'S FIRST SCHOOL

Ringo was just five years old when he began his primary school education here, although the modern school you see now replaced the original Victorian school Ringo attended. He got off to a shaky start. On his very first day he came home for lunch at mid-day and told his mother that he didn't have to go back that day. She believed him...until she spotted all the other kids returning to school!

When he was almost seven his education suffered a serious setback. An attack of appendicitis worsened into peritonitis forcing him to spend a year away from school. Luckily, he had a close childhood friend, Marie Maguire, who helped him to catch up. Now Marie Crawford she is, appropriately, an official BeatleGuide as well as Godmother to Zak, Ringo and Maureen's first child.

In 1999 RIngo made a donation to his old school to help create an activity centre for the pupils.

DINGLE VALE SECONDARY MODERN *(now Shorefields City Learning Centre) Dingle Vale, Liverpool, 8*
RINGO'S SECONDARY SCHOOL

Ringo's school, from the ages of 11 to 15, although the final two years were again spent in hospital or at home. Not surprisingly, he left without any qualifications.

When he approached the school for an end-of-school report for use as a reference in his search for a job, he claimed that it was so long since he'd last been there that nobody could remember him. Ironically, when Ringo hit the big time, the school dragged out 'his' desk at one of their open days and charged visitors for the privilege of sitting in it!

Ringo hated the school dinners here and opted for a Hovis loaf with the middle scooped out and stuffed with chips.

37 AIGBURTH DRIVE
Sefton Park, Liverpool 17
STUART SUTCLIFFE'S HOME, NOW BLENHEIM LODGE HOTEL

Stu Sutcliffe, who preceded Paul McCartney as the Beatles' bass player, lived in Flat 1 in this handsome Victorian villa overlooking Sefton Park lake. Stu was born in Edinburgh on 23rd June 1940 but the Sutcliffe family subsequently moved to Liverpool. He was already showing great artistic promise as a student at the Liverpool College of Art when he left here to move into a flat at 7 Percy Street near the college.

After his second trip to Hamburg with the Beatles, Stu decided to stay there with his German photographer girlfriend, Astrid Kerchherr, and study under Eduardo Paolozzi at the State Art College in the city. The following year, on 10 April 1962, he died of a cerebral haemorrhage in Astrid's arms as an ambulance sped them to hospital. Ironically, National Museums Liverpool has in its collection a letter sent to Stu's mother from the consultant surgeon at Liverpool's Smithdown General Hospital who was handling his case. Stu had failed to turn up for an x-ray but the consultant didn't seemed concerned. His impression was that Stu's symptoms were simply of a nervous origin. Seven months later Stu was dead.

South Liverpool

As children, each of the Beatles would have played in Sefton Park, arguably the most popular of Liverpool's grand Victorian parks. George had a passionate interest in gardening and made a substantial donation towards the restoration of the Palm House. Sefton Park was also where John's mother Julia met Freddie, his father.

SEFTON GENERAL HOSPITAL *(now Asda supermarket)*
Smithdown Road, Liverpool 15
JULIAN LENNON'S BIRTHPLACE

Birthplace, on Monday 8th April 1963, of John Charles Julian Lennon – John after his famous father, Charles after Cynthia's father and Julian, the nearest they could get to John's mother Julia. However, apart from two small units -

Smithdown Minor Injuries Centre for Children and Sefton Park Medical Centre - very little remains to remind us that this was once a large hospital. Most of the site is now taken up by an Asda supermarket.

The umbilical cord had been coiled around Julian's neck and when he made his grand entrance he was, to quote his mother, 'an awful yellow colour'. John missed all the drama; he was on tour in the South of England at the time. Two days later he was back on Merseyside playing the Majestic Ballroom in Birkenhead and saw his new son for the first time.

"Who's going to be a famous little rocker like his dad then?", John would prophetically ask the gurgling infant cradled in his arms. His visits to see Julian and Cynthia created enormous interest among staff and patients eager to catch a glimpse of the by now famous Beatle father.

But this hospital held bittersweet memories for John. Five years earlier he had rushed here by taxi to be given the devastating news that his beloved mother Julia had died following a road accident. Coincidentally, Julia's common law husband, John Dykins, also died here after being involved in a traffic accident in 1966. Their two daughters, John's half-sisters Julia and Jacqui, were also born here.

93 GARMOYLE ROAD
off Smithdown Road, Liverpool 15
CYNTHIA LENNON'S FLAT

Cynthia and Paul's girlfriend, Dot, both rented adjacent rooms in this house for a short time in 1962. It has two claims to fame. Paul McCartney, who had bought engagement rings for Dot and himself, ended their relationship abruptly here one night. And Julian Lennon was conceived here. When Cynthia broke the news of her pregnancy to John he was horrified but, as was the fashion in those days, he readily agreed to 'do the right thing'…"There's only one thing for it, Cyn, we'll have to get married."

"Penny Lane...there beneath the blue suburban skies"

PENNY LANE *Liverpool 18*

Here it is! The 'street' made famous in The Beatles' masterpiece *Penny Lane*. The shelter in the middle of the roundabout, the barber shop, the bank…they are all here, sometimes even beneath blue suburban skies.

If you stand here long enough, you may see the banker who never wears a mac or even the pretty nurse selling poppies from a tray. However, you will probably stand a better chance of seeing a fireman with his clean machine; perhaps he'll even have an hourglass and a picture of the Queen. The local fire station is only a short distance away.

John explained that when he wrote this song with Paul he was re-living his childhood. He lived in Newcastle Road, just around the corner from Penny Lane, for the first five years of his life. Daily for another six years he walked down Penny Lane to and from school. As a mischievous schoolboy he rode on the bumpers of the tramcars and did some petty thieving from the shops in Penny Lane. Later, with his group the Quarry Men, he played gigs at St Barnabas Church Hall in Penny Lane. Penny Lane was very much 'in his eyes and in his ears'.

An exasperated Liverpool City Council long ago gave up replacing the heavy metal Penny Lane name signs removed by souvenir hunters. Now the name is simply painted on the wall. In spite of this, strangers often have difficulty finding this street, the narrowest of six roads that all come together at what Liverpudlians call 'the Penny Lane roundabout'.

As an art student, Cynthia whiled away the summer holidays serving behind the cosmetics counter of the Woolworths store here. On one occasion when she was shopping in Penny Lane she was gripped by labour pains…Julian Lennon was about to make his entrance into the world.

At St.Barnabas Church on 29th May 1982, Paul's brother Mike, formerly Mike McGear of The Scaffold, married the lovely Rowena Horne. Paul, who had once been a choirboy at St.Barnabas, was the best man.

South Liverpool

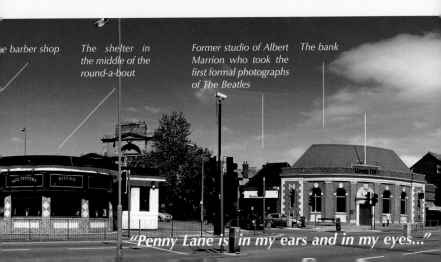

e barber shop

The shelter in the middle of the round-a-bout

Former studio of Albert Marrion who took the first formal photographs of The Beatles

The bank

"Penny Lane is in my ears and in my eyes…"

ST. BARNABAS CHURCH HALL
Penny Lane, Liverpool 18

The Quarry Men played here as an interval skiffle group at a number of Saturday night dances in the late 50's. Although St.Barnabas Church is situated at the 'Penny Lane Roundabout', this one-time church hall, now called *Dovedale Towers* and no longer connected with the church, is half way down the road.

Opposite is the Penny Lane 'Chippy' ("Penny Lane is in my eyes, a four of fish and finger pies") and the Penny Lane Cake Shop.

"I have three recollections of Dovedale Road Infants School: the smell of boiled cabbage, a little girl who had blond curly hair and a Peter Pan house in the corner of the room, made by all the kids." George

South Liverpool

DOVEDALE ROAD JUNIOR SCHOOL *off Penny Lane, Liverpool 18*
JOHN AND GEORGE'S INFANT AND JUNIOR SCHOOL

John first enrolled at Dovedale Road Infants School here on 6th May 1946. The 'Literary Lennon' quickly emerged and soon he was reading and writing fluently. Although he was inspired by books such as *Alice in Wonderland*, *Wind in the Willows* and *Just William*, John was an original thinker – "He won't do anything stereotyped" said his Headmaster. Even at that early age John himself recognised that somehow he was 'different' from the other kids.

He was just seven when he wrote his first 'book' – *Sport, Speed and Illustrated*. It saw the emergence of his distinctive style of jokes, drawings and stories alongside pasted-in images of film stars and footballers. Indeed, the sleeve of John's *Walls and Bridges* album features paintings of footballers and Red Indians done by him in his final term here in June 1952 when he was 11 years old.

Although he didn't know it at the time, there was another younger little boy with latent special talents at Dovedale at the same time as John. His name was George Harrison. John transferred to the Junior Boys School here in 1948 and finally left Dovedale for Quarry Bank Grammar School after he'd passed his '11-plus' exam in 1952. A few years later, George passed the same examination and joined Paul at the Liverpool Institute.

John enjoyed the six years he spent at this school and brought Yoko here when he first took her on a tour of his old Liverpool haunts. Later, Yoko made a number of donations to help pay for a new playground and equipment and visited the school in July 2001.

Other famous pupils include comedian Jimmy Tarbuck, television newsreader Peter Sissons and science fiction author Clive Barker.

9 NEWCASTLE ROAD *Liverpool 15*
JOHN'S FIRST HOME

Just around the corner from Penny Lane, this is the house where John was conceived and where he lived from the time he was a few days old until he was about five. Then he moved a few miles away to 'Mendips' to continue being cared for by his Aunt Mimi and Uncle George.

This was the home of the Stanley family. John's mother, Julia, was a tall, vivacious red head and the youngest of George ('Pop') and Annie Stanley's five daughters. She was also spirited, fun-loving and unconventional.

She married Freddie Lennon, a ship's waiter in the Merchant Navy, on the 3rd December 1938. They spent their 'honeymoon' at the Trocadero Cinema in London Road. At the end of the film Julia returned here and Freddie went back to his lodgings, sailing off the next day on a three-month trip to the West Indies. When John was 18 months old, Freddie left him and Julia for good. Shortly afterwards, unable to cope, Julia had virtually 'given' John to her sister Mary (Mimi) to raise.

A wartime affair with a soldier resulted in another baby which she immediately arranged to have adopted. After the war, Julia lived here with her new man, John 'Bobby' Dykins (John nicknamed him 'Twitchy') whom she'd

"That's the first place I remember (Newcastle Road). It's a good way to start - red brick; front room never used, always curtains drawn, picture of a horse and carriage on the wall. There were only three bedrooms upstairs, one on the front of the street, one in the back, and one teeny little room in the middle."
John (1979)

"I had a happy, healthy childhood in Liverpool and I like it. It doesn't stop you living somewhere else or going somewhere else, it's still my home town." John

met whilst working for a time as a waitress at a café in Penny Lane. They and their daughter, also Julia, moved to 1 Blomfield Road in 1949, the year that their second daughter, Jacqueline, was born.

MOSSPITS LANE PRIMARY SCHOOL *Mosspits Lane, Liverpool 15*
JOHN'S FIRST SCHOOL

Contrary to what is stated in many Beatle and Lennon books, this, not Dovedale Road Primary School, was the very first school attended by John.

He enrolled here on 12th November 1945 and the school's Admission Book shows his address as 9 Newcastle Road and his parent/guardian as his father Alfred. John remained here for no longer than six months since, by 6th May 1946, he had moved to Dovedale Road Infants School near Penny Lane.

12 ARNOLD GROVE *Wavertree, Liverpool 15*
GEORGE'S BIRTHPLACE

Birthplace on 25th February 1943 of the youngest Beatle, George Harrison. He lived in this cramped little house with an outside lavatory (rent 50 pence a week) for nearly seven years with his sister Louise, brothers Harold and Peter and mother and father, Louise and Harold. As George later recalled - "Our house was very small. Two up and two down - straight in off the pavement, step right out of the back room. The front room was never used. It had the posh lino and a three-piece suite and was freezing cold and nobody ever went in it. We'd all be huddled together in the kitchen, where the fire was, with the kettle on, and a little iron cooking stove."

"Arnold Grove was a bit like Coronation Street...It was behind the Lamb Hotel in Wavertree. There was a big art-deco cinema there called the Abbey, and the Picton clock tower. Down a little cobbled lane was the slaughter house, where they used to shoot horses."

George

"My earliest recollection is of sitting on a pot at the top of the stairs having a poop – shouting, Finished!" George

When George was five he enrolled at Dovedale Road Primary School. His elder brother Peter was already there, in the same class as John Lennon.

George's mother and father, a bus driver and former steward on White Star liners sailing from the Pier Head, had been on the housing waiting list for 18 years when they finally got the news that they'd been allocated a brand new Council house in Speke. They packed up all their belongings and left here the day after New Year's Day 1950.

George was christened (as 'Georgius Harrison' according to the baptism record which is in Latin) in *Our Lady of Good Help* Roman Catholic church, in nearby Chestnut Grove. His maternal grandmother lived in the next street to George at 9 Albert Grove and he recalled running through the 'jiggers' or 'back entries' to visit her.

ALLERTON / WOOLTON AREA

197 QUEEN'S DRIVE *Liverpool 18*
BRIAN EPSTEIN'S HOUSE

This is the comfortable home in one of the city's more affluent suburbs into which Brian Epstein was born in 1934. His parents, Harry and Queenie, had moved into their new five-bedroomed detached house shortly after they married a year previously.

The Epstein family had run a furniture store in Liverpool's Walton Road since the beginning of the century. When he left school in 1950, virtually an academic failure, Brian reluctantly joined the family business. Although he had set his heart on becoming an actor, and had even studied for a time at the Royal Academy of Dramatic Art (RADA), it was not to be. Eventually, he channelled his energy and artistic talent into the family furniture and record stores with remarkable success.

To mark Paul's 21st birthday on 18th June 1963, Brian and his family hosted a morning cocktail party in the lounge of this house. Later that same day at another party held for Paul at his Aunty Jin's house at 147 Dinas Lane, Huyton, John beat up Cavern DJ Bob Wooler for insinuating that he was having a homosexual affair with Brian.

John, who lived not too far away from here, was a regular visitor, sitting with Brian in the morning room as they planned The Beatles' career.

QUARRY BANK, JOHN'S GRAMMAR SCHOOL
(Now Calderstones School), Harthill Road, Liverpool 18

Almost from that day in September 1952 when he first entered the Tudor-style Quarry Bank, formerly a mansion built by a local timber merchant, John was to be the bane of his teachers' lives and the despair of his Aunt Mimi. End of term school reports provide the clue – "Hopeless. Rather a clown in class. A shocking report. He is just wasting other pupils' time. Certainly on the road to failure."

His best subject was class anarchy of which he was the undisputed leader. Fighting, smoking 'loosies' (cigarettes bought in one's and two's by those who couldn't afford a full packet), disrupting classes, canings, refusing to conform and even being banned from school, were the tarnished hallmarks of an undistinguished five-year academic career at Quarry Bank. He left on 24 July 1957 after failing all his O Level examinations, even in his favourite subject, art.

Paradoxically, his Quarry Bank days were creatively, if not academically, productive. School exercise books were filled with highly original and hilariously funny stories, poems, drawings and cartoons. One called *The Daily Howl* which mercilessly parodied his teachers was passed under the desks from one giggling schoolboy to the next. A weather report read – 'Tomorrow will be Muggy followed by Tuggy, Wuggy and Thuggy.' A cartoon showed a blind man with glasses leading a blind dog, also with glasses; the physically afflicted were frequently the butt of his humour. This early work was to form the basis for his acclaimed books *In His Own Write* and *A Spaniard in the Works*.

Quarry Bank school: the old school building is on the right. On the left is the school hall where John and his Quarry Men skiffle group played their first gig in October 1956.

"The Quarry Men is the name of the group before it turned into The Beatles. The original group was named after my school, which was Quarry Bank and had a Latin motto which meant 'out of this rock' - that's symbolic - 'you will find truth." John. He's in the centre of the group above.

It was also at Quarry Bank that John formed his first band, the Quarry Men, who were in essence a skiffle group made up of his classroom cronies. For his parting shot, John had fronted the Quarry Men at the end of term school dance held here in July 1957.

Like his predecessor, John's headmaster, Mr Pobjoy, failed to 'knock him into shape' but John did credit him for getting him into art college. So, it was a case of 'Goodbye Quarry Bank and hello Liverpool College of Art' and the bohemian life of an art student!

STRAWBERRY FIELD *Beaconsfield Road, Liverpool 25*

A short distance up the hill on the right hand side, look out for the old sandstone gate pillars inscribed 'Strawberry Field', the ornate strawberry coloured gates and the closed-off pathway leading to...'Strawberry Fields Forever'. Just stand there quietly and soak up the atmosphere of the place that inspired John Lennon to write his haunting masterpiece of pop imagery.

Opened as a Salvation Army Children's Home in 1936, Strawberry Field was a large Victorian mansion set in extensive grounds. It was demolished in the late 60's and the land at the rear sold off to help pay for the newer buildings you see today.

Often as a young boy, John would come here with his Aunt Mimi to join in the fun of the Summer Fete. It clearly held a special place in his heart. His association with Strawberry Field was a long one and lasted until the home's closure. He made a donation to the appeal for the new annexe, named Lennon Court when it opened in 1979. As part of their Liverpool 'pilgrimage', Yoko and Sean visited Strawberry Field in January, 1984, to meet the staff and children.

On 9th October that year, John's birthday, a parcel arrived from Yoko. It contained a cheque for $90,000, three records, a photograph and a poem specially written by Yoko.

Through a gift of $1m from Yoko, a 'twin' Strawberry Fields was created in 1985 from a neglected tear-shaped section of Central Park, New York – John and Yoko lived nearby in the Dakota Building. On the 9th October 1998 Yoko and the Lord Mayor of Liverpool planted an oak tree there in John's honour. Yoko also collected the Freedom of the City of Liverpool scroll awarded posthumously to John in 1984. Coincidentally, Britain's first public park, designed by the great British landscape architect Joseph Paxton, at Birkenhead, across the river from Liverpool, was used as the model by the great American parks pioneer Frederick Olmstead to create New York's Central Park.

Beatle fans worldwide were horrified when, in May 2000, thieves made off with the gates in broad daylight. They were recovered from a scrap metal dealer who had bought them in good faith only later to hear media reports of their significance. The police were alerted and the gates soon reinstated.

Sadly for Strawberry Field, times change and the trend has increasingly been for children to be cared for in foster homes rather than institutions. On 31st May 2005, the inevitable happened and the gates to the world-famous children's home were finally closed forever. The fate of Strawberry Field remained undecided but it is to be hoped that whatever its future the site will reflect its significance as a place of Beatles heritage and pilgrimage.

'MENDIPS' 251 MENLOVE AVENUE *Liverpool 25*
JOHN'S HOUSE

As this neat, semi-detached, mock-Tudor suburban home testifies, and contrary to media mythology, John Lennon, the 'Working Class Hero', did *not* come from 'the slums of Liverpool'.

Left: John standing in the porch at 'Mendips' and, right, the lounge where John would sit composing poetry and the lyrics of songs destined to be hits for The Beatles.

The Second World War had just ended when John came to 'Mendips' to be brought up by his Aunt Mimi and her dairy farmer husband, George. It was to be John's home until Beatle fame forced him to move to London in 1963. This was John's home from the age of five until he was 23. He spent more time here than anywhere else in his 40-year life. Right until the end of his life 'Mendips' held a special place in John's heart.

It was here that he had been smitten by the rock and roll bug after hearing Elvis's 'Heartbreak Hotel' on Radio Luxembourg. If the charismatic, swivel-hipped Presley ignited the spark, it was the decidedly un-hip British skiffle singer Lonnie Donegan who fanned the flame.

The whole appeal of skiffle, based on three simple guitar chords, was that it was so easy, anybody could do it. John was no exception. From the time that he carefully unwrapped his first £10 'guaranteed not to split' mail order guitar, the die was cast. From then right up to his death in 1980 he was to be a rock and roll musician.

Soon John was writing songs of his own. *The One After 909* was one early effort written whilst still at school. Other early songs written by John here in 'Mendips' include *I Call Your Name*, *Hello Little Girl* and *Please, Please Me*. John wrote this in his bedroom over the front porch. Just before his death he was to recall the exact day, even remembering the colour of the coverlet on his bed and Roy Orbison's *Only the Lonely* which, along with Bing Crosby's *Please, lend your little ears to my pleas* inspired him to write *Please, Please Me*, the first of an unbroken chain of twelve No.1 hits for The Beatles.

His authoritarian Aunt Mimi did not encourage his new-found love affair with the guitar and regularly banished him and the peace-shattering instrument out of earshot to the glazed front porch with admonition – *"The guitar's all very well John, but you'll never make a living out of it."* These immortal words were framed by American fans and took pride of place in Mimi's bungalow overlooking Poole Harbour in Dorset. John bought her this luxury home in 1965 when the attentions of the growing army of fans laying siege to 'Mendips' in the hope of a sighting of the famous Beatle became too much to take. She lived there until her death on 6th December 1991.

On account of its national importance and special interest, 'Mendips' was awarded Grade II Listed building status by English Heritage in February 2012.

Today, all that remains are the memories. But just look at 'Mendips'...and 'Imagine': The carefree childhood days John spent here with Mimi, his doting uncle George, his three cats, Titch, Tim and Sam and the family mongrel dog Sally. The frequent visits from his 'real' mother, Julia, vivacious, carefree and a kindred free spirit. Imagine John, the rebellious teenager cycling to Quarry Bank School followed by tormented art student days as the archetypal 'angry young man'. And, later, John the family man living here with his wife Cynthia and new son Julian.

Imagine too, Paul, George and Pete Best knocking on the front door to join John in early Beatles rehearsals – with Mimi well out of the way, of course! And visits from their new manager, Brian Epstein. Imagine also the times John returned to 'Mendips' drained from long nights in the seedy clubs of Hamburg, sweat-sodden from the cellar clubs of Liverpool and light-headed from tours carried along on waves of Beatlemania. Imagine it all.

And best of all, imagine, just imagine as, guitar in hand, Lennon the uncompromising genius sat on the edge of his bed (see above right) or stood in this porch (above left) creating and singing some of those classic songs for which The Beatles will forever be remembered.

On 9th December 2000, the 20th anniversary of John's death, an English Heritage blue plaque was unveiled by John's cousin and half-sister. Even more important, 'Mendips' was 'saved for the nation' when Yoko Ono bought it in 2002 following the death of the owner and immediately donated it to The National Trust. Built in 1933, many of Mendips' art-nouveau features have been retained and the National Trust has made a fine job of restoring the house to what it would have looked like when John lived here. 'Mendips' has been open to visitors since March 2003. The National Trust organises a combined visit by mini-bus to 'Mendips' and Paul's house at 20 Forthlin Road which start and finish in Liverpool city centre. This is a truly wonderful experience and should not be missed. You are advised to book in advance.

Booking arrangements: *On-line bookings – www.nationaltrust.org.uk/beatles Telephone bookings line – 0151 427 7231. Infoline – 0844 800 4791*

MENLOVE AVENUE
THE DEATH OF A MOTHER

It was dusk on that fine summer's evening – Wednesday 15th July 1958 – as John's mother Julia stood chatting to her sister Mimi at the gate of 'Mendips'. At 10pm they waved their goodbyes. Mimi went into the house and Julia headed towards the bus stop near the Vineries on the opposite side of the dual carriageway.

As she stepped from the grassed central reservation into the second carriageway of Menlove Avenue she did not see the grey Standard Vanguard saloon car, registration number LKF 630, driven by off-duty Police Constable 126 Clague, bearing down on her in the half-light.

Minutes later John's schoolfriend Nigel Whalley hammered on Mimi's door to deliver the grim news that her sister had been involved in an accident. Mimi dashed across to where Julia lay unconscious in a pool of blood. Near the bus stop, a distance of 58 feet further back up the road, her bag and its contents poignantly marked the spot where she had been sent spinning through the air. Quickly, Mimi returned to 'Mendips' for her coat and climbed into the ambulance which sped them through the Penny Lane roundabout and on to Sefton General Hospital.

Julia was pronounced 'dead on arrival'. The autopsy report noted a large fracture at the base of her skull and other injuries.

Accounts of the tragedy were wildly contradictory. Constable Clague claimed that he had been travelling at well under 30 miles per hour, that Julia had walked into his path, that he had sounded his horn and had braked, that he had even mounted the central reservation, missing trees in the process, in a desperate bid to avoid hitting her. Two eye witnesses, a 15 year old shipping clerk and a man riding his bicycle in the same direction, told a completely different story. They both said the car was going very fast, that it did not sound its horn and that the brake lights did not come on.

The inquest, exactly one month after the accident, recorded a verdict of 'misadventure'. Constable Clague later stood trial but was acquitted.

For John, the 17 year old art student who had recently 're-discovered' the mother he had 'lost' as a child, this second loss – for good this time – was almost more than he could bear. Externally, it was expressed in heavy drinking and the aggressive and often cruel 'hard man' front that he presented to the world. Internally, his sensitive feelings were later to find an outlet in songs such as *Julia* and the heart-rending *Mother* - "You had me but I never had you."

Just imagine...

16-year old John Lennon is fronting his skiffle group, the Quarry Men. In the audience is 15-year old Paul McCartney. It is the first time in his life he has clapped eyes on John but it was a moment he would never forget –

"I remember when we first met, at Woolton, at the village fete. It was a beautiful summer day and I walked in there and saw you on stage. And you were singing 'Come Go With Me' by the Del Vikings. But you didn't know the words so you made them up..." Paul

"That was the day, the day I met Paul that it started moving." John

The time: Saturday, 6th July, 1957

The place: The field at the rear of St Peter's Church, Woolton.

The occasion: The church's Summer fete and the historic first meeting of Lennon and McCartney, the 20th century's two most famous singer/songwriters.

ST. PETER'S CHURCH *Church Road, Woolton, Liverpool 25*. JOHN MEETS PAUL FOR THE FIRST TIME – 'WHERE IT ALL BEGAN'

This is the unlikely setting for the historic first meeting of the 20th century's two most famous singer/songwriters. On Saturday, 6th July 1957, the 15 year old Paul McCartney, wearing his flash white sport coat and black drainpipe trousers, cycled from his home in Allerton to St. Peter's. He'd come at the suggestion of Ivan Vaughan, a class-mate, to see the Quarry Men, a skiffle group for which Ivan sometimes played tea chest bass. And, there might also be the chance of chatting up some girls.

That afternoon, in a field behind the church, John Lennon and his Quarry Men Skiffle Group sang their way through skiffle standards like *Railroad Bill*, *Cumberland Gap* and *Maggie May*, as well as rockers such as *Be Bop A Lula* and hits of the day like the Dell Vikings's *Come Go With Me*. Paul was mightily impressed even though John had stumbled over the words of every song and had to improvise.

Afterwards, in the church hall across the road (above right) where the Quarry Men had been booked to play an evening gig, he was introduced to the group by Ivan Vaughan. Paul showed them how he played *Twenty Flight Rock*, *Be Bop a Lula* and other songs from his repertoire. Not only did Paul know all the words but he could play proper chords *and* tune a guitar, a skill that had thus far eluded John Lennon.

Paul later recalled their first meeting..."I remember this beery old man getting nearer and breathing down me neck as I was playing. 'What's this old drunk doing?' I thought. Then he said *Twenty Flight Rock* was one of his favourites. So I knew he was a connoisseur. It was John. He'd just had a few beers. He was 16 and I was only 14 (just 15 actually), so he was a big man". "I remember him in a checked shirt with slightly curly hair and I thought: He looks good – I wouldn't mind being in a group with him." Years later, John was to say "That was the day, the day I met Paul that it started moving."

Although John had more or less decided that day that he wanted him in the Quarry Men, it was a week or so before the message was finally passed to Paul – "D'ya wanna join me group?" And it wasn't until 18 October that Paul eventually made his debut with the Quarry Men.

On the 40th anniversary of John and Paul's first encounter a weekend of special celebrations was held here. There was a garden fete, a memorabilia sale, John's original band, The Quarry Men, reformed and played a gig and a commemorative plaque (see right) was unveiled at the end of a special church service at St Peter's. The Queen, Prime Minister, John's two wives and Paul were amongst the many who sent personal messages. The church hall's stage, where John and Paul played, is now on display in the Museum of Liverpool.

174 MACKETS LANE *Hunts Cross, Liverpool 25*
GEORGE'S HOUSE

The Harrison family lived here between 1962 and 1965 during which time George and The Beatles soared to worldwide fame.

Like the other Beatle houses in the 60's this Council house became the focal point for George's fans. Fan mail by the sackload was delivered and often the fans themselves turned up on the doorstep in the hope of a 'sighting'. Finally, in 1965, George's father quit his bus driver's job and the Harrisons moved into a house bought for them by George near Warrington.

1 BLOMFIELD ROAD *Liverpool 19*
JULIA LENNON'S HOUSE

Unbeknown to John for a number of years, this is the house where his real mother Julia lived. It is less than two miles away from where he lived with her sister, his Aunt Mimi, who to all intents and purposes had been his mother since he was a toddler.

The 1940's had been a turbulent period for Julia. It was wartime. She'd had a baby, John, been deserted by her sailor husband Freddie, 'given' John away to her sister to be brought up and had another wartime baby by a soldier. This child, Victoria, was born in the 'Elmswood' Nursing Home, North Mossley Hill Road, Liverpool, in June 1945 and had immediately been adopted by a Norwegian and taken to Norway.

After the war Julia had formed a steady relationship with John 'Bobby' Dykins, a head waiter in a Liverpool hotel, and had two daughters, Julia and Jacqueline, by him. It was a relationship that was to last for the rest of her life, even though it was never formalised by marriage; Julia never got round to divorcing Freddie Lennon.

During John's teenage years 1 Blomfield Road virtually became his second home. These were the years when he 're-discovered' his mother, although she was more like an older sister or fellow conspirator than a real mother. She was naturally musical and could play the piano and banjo and even juggle! Like John, she was a big Presley fan and even had a stray cat called Elvis.

Here, Julia taught John his first chords on a cheap 'guaranteed not to split' guitar; albeit they were banjo chords! Best of all, she never objected to John and his Quarry Men using her home for rehearsals. The bathroom, where the sound of guitar and washboard would bounce off the hard tiles, was a favourite bolthole for the young musicians.

John frequently stayed here, sometimes for days at a time. During one occasion, on 15th July 1958, a policeman knocked on the door to tell him and Bobby that Julia had been involved in a traffic accident. They rushed in a taxi to Sefton General Hospital, Smithdown Road, only to be told the horrible truth – the happy-go-lucky Julia was dead. For the devastated 17 year old John, this was the second time in his young life that he'd 'lost' his mother, this time for good.

ALLERTON CEMETERY *Allerton Road, Liverpool 19*
JULIA'S GRAVE

This is the final resting place of John's adored mother, Julia Lennon. She was buried here in Church of England Section 38, grave No.805, at 10am on Monday, 21st July 1958. She was 44 years of age, a woman in the prime of her life. The grave, which is unmarked, is a private one and Julia is the only member of the family buried there.

20 FORTHLIN ROAD *Allerton, Liverpool 18*
PAUL'S HOUSE *(Now owned by The National Trust)*

The McCartney family had moved house many times over the years but it was definitely a step up in the world when, in 1955, they moved from the tough Speke housing estate to Forthlin Road in the genteel leafy suburb of Allerton.

Mrs McCartney was delighted with her new home and was over the moon when her two sons won places to the Liverpool Institute, arguably the best grammar school in the city. Her joy was to be very short-lived. Along came 'Maxwell with his silver hammer' and she died of breast cancer after a short illness on 31st October 1956, leaving husband Jim to bring up Paul and his younger brother Mike. Mary's grave can be found in Yew Tree Cemetery, Section 3A, Grave 276. Tragically, Paul's wife Linda was also to fall victim to breast cancer in 1998. With Paul's backing, the Linda McCartney Centre, which provides specialist treatment for breast and others cancers, was opened two years later at the Royal Liverpool University Hospital.

In this house Paul was to 'lose' himself in his guitar, even taking it to the bathroom where the excellent acoustics compensated for the lack of an amplifier. After Paul's historic first encounter with John Lennon at the Woolton Parish Church Garden Fete on 6 July 1957, this house became a favourite rehearsal venue for the newly-formed, but soon to be formidable, Lennon and McCartney song-writing partnership. They wrote about 20 songs here, including *I Saw Her Standing There*, before their first single *Love Me Do* gave them chart success.

Unlike John's Aunt Mimi, Paul's dad was himself no mean musician and actively encouraged the boys. In any case he was at work all day in the Liverpool Cotton Exchange. And when the cat's away... and play they certainly did. Here, in the front room of this house, Paul and John, sitting opposite each other with acoustic guitars in hand, would collaborate on the dozens of songs to be written down in school exercise books: 'Another Lennon / McCartney original'. At other times they would draw each other, raid the larder, bring girls back and even smoke Typhoo tea in Jim's pipe!

73

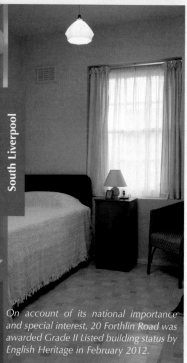

Above: the lounge, or 'front room', a favourite place for Paul and John to hang out. Left: Paul's bijou bedroom, the smallest in the house.

After the Beatles returned from their triumphant American tour in 1964, Paul bought his dad 'Rembrandt', a very 'des res' in Baskervyle Road in posh Heswall on the Wirral. With a removal van ordered for midnight, the Macs avoided the attentions of fans, media and curious neighbours by doing a moonlight flit.

Because of its importance in the history of popular music, The National Trust bought this house when it came on the market in 1996. This was a controversial 'first' for the Trust which is noted for rescuing great historic houses and grand country estates rather than humble suburban council houses. Much altered over the years, the house has been restored to what it looked like when Paul lived here. Visitors are treated to an exhibition of brother Mike's nostalgic photographs of family life at Forthlin Road, an audio tour and a display of Beatles memorabilia. A visit is highly recommended. For details of The National Trust's mini-bus tours, which include joint entry to 20 Forthlin Road and 'Mendips', see p66.

On account of its national importance and special interest, 20 Forthlin Road was awarded Grade II Listed building status by English Heritage in February 2012.

South Liverpool

FORMER WILSON HALL *Speke Road, Garston, Liverpool 19*
GEORGE'S FIRST MEETING WITH JOHN AND THE QUARRY MEN

Re-built as a Lennon's supermarket (no relation!), and now the Woolton Carpet Centre, this was the site of Wilson Hall where the Quarry Men played four times to a largely local audience of Teddy boy roughnecks.

More significantly, it was here, on 6th February 1958, that an embryonic 14 year old teddy boy by the name of George Harrison first saw the Quarry Men and was introduced to their leader John Lennon.

LIVERPOOL JOHN LENNON AIRPORT

This was The Beatles' local airport. However, the terminal building they used in those days, some distance away in Speke Road, opposite the retail park, is now an hotel.

In 1962 The Beatles flew from here to London to record *Love Me Do*, their first chart success. But the highlight for the airport came on 10th July 1964 when The Beatles flew in to a 'proper' airport reception of the kind previously witnessed at London's Heathrow and New York's John F Kennedy airports, complete with screaming fans and a press reception.

Liverpool Airport became the first in the UK to be named after an individual when, in July 2001, Yoko Ono visited the airport to announce its renaming as 'Liverpool John Lennon Airport'. Ringo later quipped that he'd like to have one of the baggage handling conveyor belts named after him!

In March 2002 Yoko returned to the Airport to unveil a 7ft bronze statue of John Lennon by local sculptor Tom Murphy. The imposing statue is sited on the main passenger walkway overlooking the check-in hall.

Outside the airport's terminal building is another reminder to visitors that Liverpool is 'Beatle City', a giant replica of the Yellow Submarine.

72 WESTERN AVENUE *Speke, Liverpool 24*
PAUL'S HOUSE

The McCartneys moved to this new council housing estate from their flat in Sir Thomas White Gardens, Everton, when Paul was four. Among the tricks he and brother Mike got up to was to throw stones at their neighbour's tree 'to speed up the growth of the apples'!

Paul's mother, Mary, worked locally as a midwife whilst father Jim was a cotton salesman for the Liverpool firm of A. Hannay and Co. He was an accomplished musician and during his inter-war bachelor years had led Jim Mac's Band.

STOCKTON WOOD ROAD PRIMARY SCHOOL
All Saints Road, Speke, Liverpool 24
PAUL'S FIRST SCHOOL

A short walk from Paul's home in Western Avenue, this was his first school. The post-war 'baby boom' pushed the school population over the 1,500 saturation level making it the biggest infants school in England, at which stage Paul and his brother Mike were moved to the Joseph Williams Primary School in Gateacre. The original school buildings have now been replaced.

12 ARDWICK ROAD
Speke, Liverpool 24
PAUL'S HOUSE

After Western Avenue, the McCartneys moved to this new Council house before leaving the sprawling Speke Council estate for Forthlin Road in 1955. Living just around the corner from here in Upton Green was George who often travelled on the same bus as Paul to their school, the Liverpool Institute. George recalled - "So Paul and I used to be on the same bus, in the same school uniform, travelling home from the Liverpool Institute. I discovered that he had a trumpet and he found out that I had a guitar, and we got together. I was about thirteen."

25 UPTON GREEN *Speke, Liverpool 24*
GEORGE'S HOUSE

The Harrison family had been on Liverpool Corporation's housing waiting list for 18 years when, the day after New Year's Day 1950, they at last moved to this new house. Compared with their tiny 'two up, two down' house in a back street cul-de-sac in Wavertree, this house must have seemed palatial. And there was a 'green' where children could play safely under the watchful eyes of their mothers.

George was six years old at the time and this was to be his home until 1 October 1962 when the family moved to Mackets Lane in Hunts Cross, a posher part of Liverpool. Luckily, George's mother positively approved of his struggle to master the guitar so this was always a favourite house for practice sessions.

At the nearby British Legion Club in Damwood Road the Rebels, featuring George and his brother Peter, played their one and only gig in 1956 for the princely sum of ten shillings (fifty pence) each.

Believe it or not but this house was also the highly unlikely setting for a Quarry Men gig – no doubt an unpaid one! The occasion? Big brother Harry's wedding reception on 20th December 1958.

"*Paul introduced me to George and I had to make the decision whether to let George in. I listened to him play and said 'Play Raunchy'. I let him in and that was the three of us then, and the rest of the group was thrown out, practically.*" John

South Liverpool

North and East Liverpool

NORTH AND EAST LIVERPOOL

1. The Collegiate
2. Grafton & Locarno
3. Beatle Streets
4. 10 Sunbury Road
5. Walton Hospital
6. Jewish Cemetery
7. Casbah Club
8. Broadway Con' Club
9. Lathom Hall
10. Litherland Town Hall
11. Huyton Parish Church Cemetery

78

FORMER COLLEGIATE *Shaw Street, Liverpool 6*
PETE BEST'S GRAMMAR SCHOOL

The Collegiate vied with the Liverpool Institute for the reputation of being the best grammar school in the city. Pete Best was a sixth form student here, leaving in 1958. The following year he met the frequently drummerless Quarry Men – John, Paul and George – and the year after that he finally joined The Beatles for their first trip to Hamburg. The Collegiate has been redeveloped into private apartments for inner city living; happily the imposing original facade of the building has been retained.

North & East Liverpool

THE GRAFTON AND LOCARNO BALLROOMS

West Derby Road, Liverpool 6

The 'Loc', and next door neighbour, the 'Gravvie' (now re-named the Olympia) – affectionately known for its 'Grab-a-granny' nights – were two of a number of large, popular 'palais de dance' venues on the fringe of the city centre where the Quarry Men and later The Beatles played during the late 50's and early 60's.

When The Beatles first performed at the 'Loc' on 14th February 1963 at a special St. Valentine's Night dance, they had already recorded their *Please, Please Me* album. They appeared four times at the 'Gravvie', their parting gig taking place on 2nd August 1963. This was to be their final Merseyside dance hall date. The following night would see their last-ever appearance at the Cavern.

In 1983 Paul invited me to meet him on the set of *Give My Regards To Broad Street*. It was a big thrill to watch the filming of his terrific rocker *Ballroom Dancing*, no doubt inspired by the likes of the 'Gravvie' and the 'Loc'.

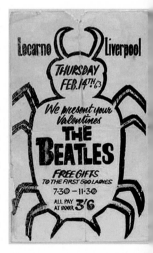

'BEATLE STREETS' *Kensington Fields Estate, Liverpool 6*

After long and intensive campaigning by a small band of stalwart local Beatle fans, the Council reluctantly agreed to name four of the streets on this 1981 private housing estate after The Beatles.

As well as John Lennon Drive, Paul McCartney Way, George Harrison Close and Ringo Starr Close, there are Epstein Court, Apple Court and Cavern Court. Nearby, and coincidentally, you will find Sutcliffe Street, although this is an old Liverpool street with no real link to Stuart Sutcliffe. A number of owners have given their houses Beatles-type names.

10 SUNBURY ROAD *Anfield, Liverpool 4*
PAUL'S FIRST HOUSE

Jim and Mary McCartney moved into furnished rooms here after their wartime wedding in April 1941. It was to this house in June of the following year that the newly-born Paul was brought from Walton Hospital.

Soon, however, the McCartneys were on the move again, first to 92 Broadway Avenue, Wallasey, then to a pre-fabricated bungalow at Roach Avenue, Knowsley, on the outskirts of Liverpool. Then it was back to the city centre to a ground floor flat in Sir Thomas White Gardens, Everton, followed by a move to the giant new Speke estate and another two houses before the restless McCartneys settled in Forthlin Road, their last Liverpool home.

WALTON HOSPITAL *Rice Lane, Liverpool 9*
(now part of Aintree Hospitals)
PAUL'S BIRTHPLACE

Birthplace of Beatle Paul or, to give him his full name, James Paul McCartney. Paul's mother, Mary, had once been a sister on the maternity ward here and had qualified for a private ward for the birth of Paul, her first child, on 18th June 1942. Both of Paul's parents were in their thirties when they married – Jim was 39, Mary 32. Paul's brother Peter, but known for most of his life as Mike, was also born here, on 7th January 1944.

Paul's birth certificate was sold at a Bonham's auction in Tokyo in March 1997 for a staggering £51,715. Paul was understandably miffed to put it mildly that, quite literally, his birthright had been 'stolen' from under him.

JEWISH CEMETERY *Long Lane, Aintree, Liverpool 9*
BRIAN EPSTEIN'S GRAVE

Following his tragic death at his London flat from an overdose of the drug Carbrital on 27 August 1967 at the age of 32, Brian Epstein's body was carried from Liverpool's Greenbank Drive Synagogue and buried here in Grave H12, Section A.

Along with the Epstein family at the graveside ceremony at 7pm on 29 August were Brian's favourites – Cilla Black, Gerry (of Gerry and the Pacemakers) and Nat Weiss, his American friend and lawyer. In defiance of the Jewish rule forbidding flowers at funerals, Weiss tossed a newspaper containing a single hidden white chrysanthemum onto Brian's coffin, a farewell request from George on behalf of The Beatles.

Brian's father, mother and brother are also buried here.

8 HAYMAN'S GREEN *West Derby, Liverpool 12*
PETE BEST'S HOUSE & CASBAH COFFEE CLUB

On 29th August 1959, as the Quarry Men, John, Paul and George performed at the opening night of this social club for teenagers created in the basement of Mona Best's rambling Victorian house. From then until June 1962 they played 44 gigs at the Casbah.

Mona's son had also been smitten by the rock and roll bug and played drums with his Blackjacks group. His name was Pete Best and by August 1960 he had joined The Beatles as their new drummer on their first trip to Hamburg.

Two years later, on 16th August 1962, to the fury of his many fans, he was unceremoniously dumped by The Beatles in favour of Ringo Starr. Too good looking? Not up to the mark as a drummer? Didn't fit in with the other Beatles? No convincing explanation has ever been given for this 'knife in the back' episode and to this day Pete Best is adamant that he still doesn't know why he was sacked. Suffice it to say that none of the Beatles had the guts to tell Pete to his face; they left the dirty work to Brian. Less than a month later they had recorded *Love Me Do* and were on their way to fame and fortune leaving behind a devastated Pete Best. Happily, Pete did not allow this crushing blow to embitter him for long.

Earlier that same year, on 24th January 1962, Pete, along with John, Paul and George, had gathered here for the formal signing of Brian Epstein's management contract.

Certainly to his girl fans, Pete, with his dark, moody film star looks, was far and away the 'best' of The Beatles. It was not unknown for love-struck teenage girls to sleep in the front garden here simply to be near him.

"It was great to be involved in the birth of a coffee bar - they were such important places then. The concrete and wood in the basement had been stripped and we painted each part a different colour. All of us lent a hand - John and George and all the others. And after we'd painted it up, it was our club The Beatles used to play there. Pete had a drum kit so he would sometimes sit in with us. He was a good drummer and when Hamburg came up he joined us. He was a very good-looking guy, and out of all the people in our group, the girls used to go for Pete." **Paul**

Unlike John, Paul, George and Ringo, Randolph Peter Best, to give him his full name, was born, not in Liverpool, but in Madras, India, on 24th November 1941. The family came to Liverpool at Christmas 1945, living first in a flat in Casey Street, then at 17 Queenscourt Road, West Derby, before finally settling at 8 Hayman's Green, West Derby.

Pete, a family man and retired Civil Servant, has made quite a few appearances as a guest speaker at Beatle Conventions. More interestingly, he has formed his Pete Best Band and tours extensively. Royalties from *The Beatles Anthology*, where Pete's drumming is featured on ten tracks, has meant that, over 30 years on, Pete was finally able to reap considerable financial reward from recordings made during his days with the early Beatles.

To mark the 40th anniversary of the Casbah Coffee Club in 1999, local Merseybeat-era bands performed for fans in the grounds of this house. They were also able to see ceiling and wall paintings by The Beatles and Cynthia Lennon. A replica of part of the Casbah was also installed in the Beatles Story museum at Albert Dock.

The opening night of the Casbah with the Quarry Men (left to right) George, Paul, Ken Brown and John...but no drummer.

Today, some 50 years on, the Casbah is still owned by Pete Best and is open to visitors for pre-booked guided tours. For further information and details of visiting arrangements, log on to www.casbahcoffeeclub.com

CLUBMOOR CONSERVATIVE MEN'S CLUB
Back Broadway, Liverpool 11
PAUL'S FIRST GIG WITH JOHN AND THE QUARRY MEN

Previously, as the New Clubmoor Hall, this saw Paul's very first appearance with John and the Quarry Men, on 18th October 1957. It was an occasion memorable only because Paul, on his first and virtually last instrumental solo, fluffed 'Guitar Boogie'.

LATHOM HALL *Lathom Avenue, Seaforth, Liverpool*

Once a cinema, this was yet another of the unprepossessing suburban 'jive halls' on the early Beatles circuit. It is notable for being the very first officially advertised gig for the 'Silver Beats' on 21st May 1960. However, it was one they never played since they were in Scotland on the final leg of the Johnny Gentle tour.

As the Silver Beats, they had played an interval spot the week previously and went on to play a few more engagements early in 1961. That first night base player Stu Sutcliffe had been roughed up in a fight. John and Pete Best had gone to his rescue and John ended up with a broken finger. The oft-repeated story that Stu had been kicked in the head and that this resulted in his death from a brain haemorrhage two years later in Hamburg is, according to Pete Best who witnessed the incident, a myth.

LITHERLAND TOWN HALL *Hatton Hill Road, Litherland*
BIRTHPLACE OF 'BEATLEMANIA'

Litherland Town Hall, recently the recipient of a multi-million pound make-over and now home to South Sefton NHS Trust, hosted scores of Beatles gigs during 1961.

Significantly, they had played here on one historic occasion in 1960. On 27th December, in a £6 booking arranged by Bob Wooler and billed as 'Direct from Hamburg', The Beatles brought the house down, invoking early scenes of the 'Beatlemania' that went on to sweep through the country and encircle the globe. Fame and fortune were now within their grasp.

The leather-jacketed Beatles had only played North Liverpool once before and many in the audience that night really did believe that they were a German group. Local promoter Brian Kelly knew when he was on to a good thing and immediately booked them for no less than 36 dances over the next three months. It was to establish them as Merseyside's top rock and roll band.

They played their final gig here on the evening of another historic day, 9th November 1961. As The Beatles were playing a lunchtime session at the Cavern that day, Brian Epstein came to see what all the fuss was about. As they say, the rest is history.

HUYTON PARISH CHURCH CEMETERY
Stanley Road/Blue Bell Lane, Huyton.
STU SUTCLIFFE'S GRAVE

Although Stu Sutcliffe died in Hamburg on 10th April 1962, aged 21 years, he was not, contrary to popular belief, buried there. His final resting place is in this cemetery, grave number 552 in the 1939 section.

Visitors wanting to see the grave should make prior arrangements by telephoning 0151 449 3900

The Beatles stood in the shower of their cramped dressing room at the Empire Theatre for this photograph.

BEATLE PLACES TO VISIT 'ACROSS THE WATER' IN WIRRAL

Wirral, the peninsula which lies between the River Mersey and the River Dee, is by far the most scenic of Merseyside's five 'boroughs'. Although the Mersey may seem like a barrier, two road tunnels, an underground railway, a ferryboat service and even a road and rail bridge at Runcorn, mean that travelling between Liverpool and Wirral is a breeze.

When Merseysiders want a day out on their doorstep, they head for either Wirral or Southport. When they were young The Beatles were no exception; favourite playgrounds for them were the New Brighton and Wallasey beaches.

Deceptively genteel, Wirral can lay claim to a number of Beatle 'firsts'. These include the very first time John, Paul, George and their new drummer, Ringo, performed on stage together, the first time they played in suits, the first booking organised for them by their new manager, Brian Epstein, their first ever radio interview and the first time they shared the bill with the rock and roll superstars of their day, such as Little Richard and Bruce Channel.

FORMER MAJESTIC BALLROOM *Conway Street, Birkenhead*

Now a Chinese restaurant, this was once a prestigious venue operated by the Top Rank organisation and an important one for The Beatles. They made seventeen appearances here between June 1962 and April 1963, perhaps the most memorable being on 15th December when they were crowned 1962's undisputed 'Kings of Mersey Beat' at the first *Mersey Beat* poll awards show. Runners up were Lee Curtis and the All Stars...whose drummer was the recently deposed Pete Best. The photograph overleaf shows Bill Harry, Editor of the Mersey Beat newspaper, presenting The Beatles with their trophy, the first of many the group would win in the years ahead.

Wirral

Bill Harry, Editor of the Mersey Beat newspaper, presents The Beatles with their very first trophy, The Mersey Beat Popularity Poll shield, at Birkenhead's Majestic Ballroom.

GROSVENOR BALLROOM *Grosvenor Street, Liscard, Wallasey*

Wirral

Another suburban dance hall that finally yielded, at least temporarily, under the onslaught of rock 'n' roll by the likes of Gerry and the Pacemakers and The Beatles who played here 14 times during 1960 and 1961. Memorable because the gig on 10th March 1961 was the very last one booked for them by Allan Williams a.k.a. 'The Man Who Gave Away The Beatles'.

It was also memorable for the punches which were often swung during its 'Swing Sessions'. Paul reminisced - "The Grosvenor Ballroom in Wallasey was one of the worst places; there would be a hundred Wallasey lads squaring up to a hundred lads from Seacombe and all hell would break loose. I remember one night a rumble had started before I realised what was happening. I ran to the stage to save my Elpico amp, my pride and joy at the time. There were fists flying everywhere. One Ted grabbed me and said 'Don't move, or you're bloody dead!' I was scared for my life but I had to get that amp." In those days you could book The Beatles for about £10.

FORMER TOWER BALLROOM *Promenade, New Brighton*

The Beatles played numerous gigs at this enormous ballroom between 1961 and 1963, most notably for local promoter Sam Leach's ambitious 'Operation Big Beat' shows which featured up to twelve acts on the one bill. The ballroom's sprung dance floor could easily accommodate 1,000 jiving couples.

The highlight of The Beatles' many appearances here was undoubtedly on 12th October 1962, the week after *'Love Me Do'* had been released, when they were second on the bill to one of their all-time heroes, Little Richard. Embarrassingly, the recently-ousted Pete Best was also there that night – as drummer with Lee Curtis and the All Stars. On other occasions The Beatles shared the stage with Bruce Channel, Joe Brown & his Bruvvers and, wait for it, the Clan McLeod Pipe Band!

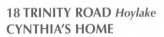

A spectacular fire in 1969 marked the final end of the Tower Ballroom and Grounds. When it opened in 1900, the 567ft tower, modelled on the Eiffel Tower, was the tallest structure in the country. There was even a Parisian Tea Garden in the grounds. However, the tower had been operating for less than 20 years when the rot started to set in; literally; it was being eaten away by rust and the entire structure was dismantled.

Wirral

18 TRINITY ROAD *Hoylake*
CYNTHIA'S HOME

This was the Powell family's modest home where Cynthia was living when she and John Lennon met at the Liverpool College of Art and embarked on a passionate teenage love affair.

Once, following a vigorous love-making session in Stu Sutcliffe' flat, she ended up in the nearby Hoylake Cottage Hospital with grumbling appendicitis. She was visited by a concerned John, although for his first visit he brought George along too! Afterwards, John and George called here to tuck into plates of egg and chips served up by Cynthia's mother.

Here Cynthia also eagerly awaited the arrival of John's letters from Hamburg described by him as "The sexiest this side of Henry Miller. Forty pages long some of them".

In between leaving 'Mendips' and finally moving to London, this was 'home' for Cynthia, Julian and John, although he was almost constantly on the road at this time. During this period John took Cynthia on a belated Parisian honeymoon. Soon after they returned, the Press discovered that they were married and laid siege to the house in the hope of a sighting of the famous Beatle with his new wife and baby Julian.

The ante-room to the gentlemen's lavatory was the makeshift studio for this local hospital radio interview when The Beatles appeared at Hulme Hall on 27th October 1962. During the interview Paul confirms that John is indeed the leader of the group.

HULME HALL *Port Sunlight Village*
'BIRTH OF THE BEATLES'

The unlikely but truly historic venue on 18th August 1962 for the real 'Birth of The Beatles'. This marked Ringo Starr's very first appearance as The Beatles' drummer. The Fab Four were complete. It was one of four gigs played in this Tudor-style village hall during 1962 for such hip bodies as the Horticultural Society, the Golf Club and the Recreations Association.

Don't leave this unique and beautiful village, created over a century ago by soap baron Lord Leverhulme, without visiting the 'jewel in the crown', the Lady Lever Art Gallery (below). It is truly exquisite and ranks among the world's top art museums. Be prepared to be impressed.

MACDONA HALL *Banks Road/ Salisbury Avenue, West Kirby*

After coming under his wing one week earlier, this was the first real booking The Beatles' new manager Brian Epstein arranged for them. The date was 1st February 1962 and Brian, in true showman style, had advertised it as the 'Grand Opening of 'The Beatle Club'. In fact, this was the only time they played here and nothing more was heard of The Beatle Club!

The gig took place in the hall used as a dance studio above Scogs restaurant which, in those days, was occupied by the Thistle Café.

BARNSTON WOMEN'S INSTITUTE
Barnston Road, Heswall

In 1962 The Beatles were booked by the Heswall Jazz Club, which held weekly jazz nights, to play in this village hall. Their first appearance, on 24th March, was something of a red letter day; they wore their new stage suits with smart shirts and matching ties for the very first time. The grey £40 suits were specially made by master tailor Beno Dorn following a visit by The Beatles and Brian Epstein to his shop in nearby Birkenhead. On 30th June, one of three gigs they played in this unlikely venue, you could have watched The Beatles and The Big Three perform live on stage *and* listen to the top 20 records of the day, all for less than £1!

THE HESWALL JAZZ CLUB

Saturday, 24th March, 1962

The Fabulous
BEATLES
(Polydor Recording Artistes)
(Mersey Beat Popularity Poll Winners)
(Prior to European Tour)

Plus

Wirral's Top Jazz Group
The Pasadena Jazzmen

Plus

The current TOP TWENTY records

★ ★

at Barnston Women's Institut

from 7-30 p.m. — 11-15 p.m.

Admission by Ticket only 7/6
No Admission after 10-0 p.m.

Wirral

'REMBRANDT' *Baskervyle Road, Heswall*

Overlooking the Dee estuary and the hills of North Wales, this is the house which Paul bought for his father for £8,750 when he returned from America after The Beatles' triumphant tour of America in 1964. Compared with their small terraced house in Forthlin Road, this five bed-roomed detached house was truly palatial.

Crippled by arthritis, Jim McCartney eventually moved to a bungalow nearby and died in March 1976. 'Rembrandt' was bought from his father by Paul and is still owned by him.

Beatles gigs venues

LIVERPOOL CITY CENTRE

Cabaret Club 28 Duke Street

Cassanova Club
The Temple, Temple Street

Cassanova Club 1st floor ballroom,
corner London Rd/Fraser Street

The Cavern 10a Mathew Street

David Lewis Theatre Great George Place

Empire Theatre Lime Street

Iron Door Club/Liverpool Jazz Society
13 Temple Street

Jacaranda Coffee Bar 23 Slater Street

Lewis's Department Store Ranelagh Street

Liverpool College of Art Hope Street

Merseyside Civil Service Club
Lower Castle Street

Odd Spot Club 89 Bold Street

Odeon Cinema London Road

Royal Iris Cruiseship River Mersey

ELSEWHERE IN AND AROUND LIVERPOOL

Aintree Institute Longmoor Lane

Albany Cinema Northway Maghull

Blair Hall Walton Road, Walton

Casbah Coffee Club
8 Hayman's Green, West Derby

Childwall Labour Club

Finch Lane Social Club
Finch Lane, Nr Huyton

Gateacre Labour Club

Grafton Ballroom
West Derby Road

Hambleton Hall St. David's Road,
Page Moss, Nr Huyton

Holyoake Hall
Smithdown Road, Nr Penny Lane

Knotty Ash Village Hall
East Prescot Road

Lee Park Golf Club
off Childwall Valley Road

Locarno Ballroom West Derby Road

Lowlands Club
Hayman's Green, West Derby

Morgue Skiffle Cellar
25 Oakhill Park, Broadgreen

Mossway Hall Moss Way, Croxteth

New Cabaret Artistes
174a Upper Parliament Street

New Clubmoor Hall
(Conservative Club)
Back Broadway

New Colony Club
80 Berkley Street

Pavilion Theatre Lodge Lane

Picton Road Bus Depot Social Club
Picton Road, Wavertree

Quarry Bank High School
Harthill Road

Rialto Ballroom
Upper Parliament Street, Toxteth

Rosebery Street Toxteth

Beatles gigs venues

St.Barnabas Church Hall Penny Lane

St.John's Hall
Snaefell Avenue, Tuebrook

St.Peter's Church Hall
Church Road, Woolton

Stanley Abattoir Social Club
East Prescot Road, Old Swan

Starline Club Windsor Street, Toxteth

25 Upton Green Speke

Wilson Hall Speke Road, Garston

Winter Gardens Ballroom
Heald Street, Garston

Woolton Village Club
Allerton Road, Woolton

CROSBY / SEAFORTH / LITHERLAND / BOOTLE

Alexandra Hall College Road, Crosby

Lathom Hall Lathom Avenue, Seaforth

Litherland Town Hall
Hatton Hill Road, Litherland

St. John's Hall Oriel Road, Bootle

St. Luke's Crosby Church Youth Club

ST HELENS / WIDNES

Town Hall, Earlestown, St Helens

Plaza Ballroom Duke Street, St Helens

Queen's Hall Widnes

SOUTHPORT

ATC Club Birkdale, Nr Southport

Cambridge Hall Lord Street

Floral Hall Promenade

Glenpark Club Lord Street

Kingsway Club Promenade

Little Theatre Hoghton Street

Odeon Cinema Lord Street

Queens Hotel Promenade

WIRRAL

Barnston Women's Institute
Barnston Road, Heswall

Ellesmere Port Civic Hall
Whitby Road, Ellesmere Port

Grosvenor Ballroom
Grosvenor Street, Wallasey

Haig Dance Club
Haig Avenue, Moreton

Hulme Hall, Port Sunlight Village

Macdona Hall/Thistle Cafe
Banks Road, West Kirby

Majestic Ballroom
Conway Street, Birkenhead

Neston Institute
Hinderton Road, Neston

Newton Dancing School
Village Hall, Thingwall Road, Irby

St.Paul's Presbyterian Church Hall
North Road, Tranmere

Technical College Hall
Borough Road, Birkenhead

Tower Ballroom
Promenade, New Brighton

YMCA Whetstone Lane,
Birkenhead

YMCA Birkenhead Road, Hoylake

Victoria Hall
Village Road, Higher Bebington.

Top Beatles Sights

1 Penny Lane

2 Strawberry Field
Beaconsfield Road, Woolton

3 St Peter's Church, Woolton
John and Paul meet for the first time

4 Mathew Street
Cavern Quarter

Beatle Birthplaces

5 John's birthplace
Maternity Hospital, Oxford Street

6 Paul's birthplace
Walton Hospital, Rice Lane

7 George's birthplace
12 Arnold Grove, Wavertree

8 Ringo's birthplace
9 Madryn Street, Dingle

Beatle Houses

9 John's house 'Mendips'
251 Menlove Avenue, Woolton

10 Paul's house
20 Forthlin Road, Allerton

11 George's house
174 Macket's Lane,
Hunts Cross

12 Ringo's house
10 Admiral Grove, Dingle

13 Pete Best's house & Casbah Club
8 Hayman's Green,
West Derby

14 Stu Sutcliffe's house
37 Aigburth Drive, Sefton Park

15 Brian Epstein's house
197 Queen's Drive, Woolton

Beatle Colleges

16 John's College of Art
Hope Street

17 Paul and George's college
Liverpool Institute, Mount Street

18 John's college
Quarry Bank Grammar School
Harthill Road, Woolton

Other Places

19 John, Paul, George and Ringo
play together for the first time as
The Beatles
Hulme Hall, Port Sunlight
Village, Wirral

20 Birthplace of local Beatlemania
Litherland Town Hall

1 Birthplace – Maternity Hospital, Oxford Street

6 Liverpool College of Art – Hope Street

2 House – 'Mendips', 251 Menlove Avenue

7 John meets Paul for the first time – St Peter's Church Hall

3 Strawberry Field – Beaconsfield Road, Woolton

8 John marries Cynthia – Mount Pleasant Registry Office

4 Infants and Junior School – Dovedale Road, Penny Lane

9 First house – 9 Newcastle Road, Penny Lane

5 College – Quarry Bank, Harthill Road, Woolton

10 Mother's house – 1 Blomfield Road, Allerton

Top Beatles Sights

"You can take the boys out of Liverpool but you can't take Liverpool out of the boys." From their first tentative efforts as budding songwriters, Lennon and McCartney were inspired by Liverpool, its people and its places. First-time visitors to the city are often surprised to find that there really is a Penny Lane and a Strawberry Field, but not an Abbey Road...that's in London!

Here are songs that had their origins in, or were inspired by, Liverpool, The Beatles' birthplace. The album on which it appears is given after each song.

Cayenne (Anthology)

A Shadows-style instrumental written by Paul at Forthlin Road when he was about 14, before he met John and not long after he'd got his first guitar.

Do You Want to Know a Secret? (Please Please Me)

Written by John after he and Cynthia moved into Brian Epstein's flat at 36 Falkner Street (above) this song has its foundation in another tune his mother sang to him as a young boy. "Want to know a secret? Promise not to tell?" warbled Snow White in the 1937 Disney classic *Snow White and the Seven Dwarfs*. The actual secret was John's realisation that he really was in love with Cynthia. The song provided Liverpudlian Billy J Kramer with a No. 1 hit in 1963.

John re-wrote the fairytale for his *Spaniard in the Works* book calling it *Snore Wife and the Several Dwarts*.

Eleanor Rigby (Revolver)

A number of theories have been put forward to explain the origins of the name Eleanor Rigby. Paul, who wrote the song, thought that 'Eleanor' came from Eleanor Bron the actress who appeared in The Beatles' *Help* whilst 'Rigby' was part of a sign 'Rigby & Evens Ltd', a firm of wine and spirit

IN LOVING MEMORY OF
MY DEAR HUSBAND
JOHN RIGBY,
WHO DEPARTED THIS LIFE
OCT 4TH 1915 AGED 72 YEARS.
"AT REST"
ALSO FRANCES, WIFE OF THE ABOVE,
DIED APRIL 3RD 1928, AGED 85 YEARS.
ALSO DORIS W. DAUGHTER OF
F & E RIGBY, DIED DEC. 24TH 1927,
AGED 2 YEARS & 3 MONTHS.
ALSO ELEANOR RIGBY
THE BELOVED WIFE OF THOMAS WOODS
AND GRANDDAUGHTER OF THE ABOVE
DIED 10TH OCT 1939, AGED 44 YEARS.
ASLEEP
ALSO FRANCES,
DAUGHTER OF THE ABOVE
DIED 2ND NOVEMBER 1949,
AGED 71 YEARS.

shippers he had noticed during a visit to Bristol. A more whimsical but unconfirmed explanation is that, perhaps subconsciously, Paul had seen the gravestone of the Eleanor Rigby who is buried in the church-yard of St Peter's Church, Woolton. The gravestone is just yards away from where Paul had first met John.

Free as a Bird (*Anthology*)

Based on a rough demo recorded by John in his New York apartment in 1977, this became the first 'new' Beatle record for 25 years. John's line – "Whatever happened to the boy that I once knew." – fits in with the concept that the song was written for a planned musical about John's life and times in the 60's.

The recording was treated by Paul, George and Ringo as though John was still alive. Paul explained: "We came up with this holiday scenario. I rang up Ringo and said let's pretend that John's gone on holiday and he's sent us a cassette and said, 'Finish it up for me'."

Directed by Joe Pytka, produced by Vincent Jolier, and principally filmed at various locations around Liverpool, the *Free as a Bird* video bristles with intriguing references to

Beatle places and songs, including *Penny Lane*, *Strawberry Fields*, *Eleanor Rigby*, *Yellow Submarine* and *I am the Walrus*. The video also includes a sequence showing a white grand piano falling from the sky and hurtling past Liverpool's most famous building, the Royal Liver Building (below left).

Golden Slumbers (*Abbey Road*)

Conceived by Paul on the piano at the house that he bought his father in Baskervyle Road, Heswall. A song-book belonging to his step-sister Ruth provided the inspiration. It contained the traditional lullaby *Golden Slumbers* by Shakespeare's contemporary, Thomas Dekker. As Paul was unable to read sheet music in those days, he made up his own melody.

"We always had a piano. (It's a great-sounding piano, which I still have. It was bought, incidentally, from North End Music Stores, NEMS. Brian Epstein was the son of Harry Epstein, the owner, and my dad bought his first piano from Harry. It is all like that in Liverpool, pretty inter-twined.)".

"I wrote 'When I'm Sixty-Four' on that when I was still sixteen..." **Paul**

Glass Onion (*The Beatles*)

Written by John to wind up all those fans who tried to outdo each other by finding hidden meanings in Beatle songs (remember the 'Paul is dead' theory?). Apart from Strawberry Fields, another Liverpool placename is mentioned – the cast iron shore or, as we call it, 'The cassie'. To describe it as a 'beach', however, would be to over-glamourise it. It was, and is, pretty disgusting but as it was the only part of Liverpool's shoreline

Liverpool & Beatles Songs

accessible to the public, it was popular with children from south Liverpool.

Hello Little Girl (*Anthology*)

John's first original song written when he was about 18. It was influenced by Buddy Holly's *Maybe Baby* and inspired by a song sung to him by his mother, a Cole Porter number *It's De-lovely* sung by Bob Hope. The song also gave another Liverpool group, The Fourmost, a number 7 hit in 1962.

Hey Jude (*The 1 Album*)

Written by Paul, it was about John and Cynthia's Liverpool-born five-year old son Julian ('Hey Jules' became *Hey Jude*) with whom Paul had always been close. John said that this was his favourite Paul song.

I Am The Walrus
(*Magical Mystery Tour*)

The catalyst for this surreal song was a letter from a pupil at John's old school, Quarry Bank, explaining that his class had been given the task of analysing the lyrics of Beatle songs. John found this ironic especially as his English teachers had given up on him…Lennon had excelled only in class anarchy. The title was inspired by the poem *The Walrus and The Carpenter* written by John's favourite author, Lewis Carroll. *The Walrus and The Carpenter* was one of ten hand-written and illustrated poems included in John's *My Anthology*, done when he was a 12 year old pupil at Quarry Bank.

The line 'I am the eggman' may have been a reference to another Lewis Carroll character, Humpty Dumpty from *Through The Looking Glass*. Another line 'Yellow matter custard dripping from a dead dog's eye' came from a playground ditty chanted by every Liverpool school-boy in the 40's, and usually directed at more sensitive souls i.e. girls – 'Yellow matter custard, green snot pie, all mixed up with a dead dog's eye. Spread it on a butty, spread it on thick, then wash it down with a cup of cold sick.' Revolting!

The Walrus crops up again on *Glass Onion* ("The Walrus was Paul.") and on the John Lennon/Plastic Ono Band track *God* ("I was the Walrus. But now I'm John").

I Lost My Little Girl

Thought to be the earliest song written by Paul, it formed part of the Quarry Men's repertoire but was dropped when the group became The Beatles.

I'll Follow The Sun (*Beatles For Sale*)

An early Paul song written it is said when he was 16 and recovering from a bout of 'flu; the inspiration for the song came as he gazed through the lace-curtained front window of his Forthlin Road home.

I'll Get You (*Past Masters: Volume 1*)

Another song written at 251 Menlove Avenue by John and Paul, the 'B' side of their mega-hit *She Loves You*.

The 'Dockers Umbrella' – the Liverpool Overhead Railway 100 years ago.

In My Life (*Rubber Soul*)

As the original scribbled lyrics reveal, this song started life as an autobiographical reflection on some of John's favourite Liverpool landmarks as he travelled from Menlove Avenue to the Pier Head. Among the places he remembered were Penny Lane, Church Road (a road that leads from Penny Lane past Newcastle Road where his first home was) and the Clock Tower (Wavertree Clock Tower). "In the circle of the Abbey. I have seen some happy hours.", is a reference to the former Abbey Cinema. "Past the tramsheds with no trams." refers to the Smithdown Road Tram Depot. "On the 5 'bus into town" is the number 5 bus that goes from Woolton, past John's house and on to Liverpool city centre (Liverpudlians have always called their city centre 'town'). "Past the Duchy (a small cafe and hangout for local teenagers) and St Columba's" (church) "To the dockers umbrella that they pulled down." relates to one of the real wonders of Liverpool and a world-first for the city that was sadly demolished in the 1950's – an overhead electric railway (see left) that ran the length of Liverpool docks from Seaforth in the north past the Pier Head finishing at Dingle (near Ringo's home) in the south. Dockers on their way to and from work would shelter under it from the rain.

John's boyhood friend, Pete Shotton, claimed John told him that when he wrote: "...friends I still can recall, some are dead and some are living,.." he was specifically thinking about former Beatle Stu Sutcliffe and Pete.

I Saw Her Standing There
(*Please Please Me*)

Refined by Paul and John in the front room of Paul's house in Forthlin Road, (above right), the song's raw beginnings came to Paul as he was

driving home one night in 1962. The lyrics were jotted down in a Liverpool Institute exercise book with Paul starting the ball rolling – "She was just seventeen" with John adding the very Liverpudlian saying – "You know what I mean."

Apparently, the inspiration for this song was Iris Caldwell, sister of Alan Caldwell, better known as Rory Storm, leader of Rory Storm and the Hurricanes whose drummer was Ringo Starr. Iris was a professional dancer and was 17 at the time Paul spotted her dancing the twist in her fishnet stockings at the Tower Ballroom, New Brighton. Paul and Iris dated on and off for a few years.

I Call Your Name
(*Past Masters: Volume 1*)

Although Paul claims to remember working on this song in John's bedroom, John reckoned that he wrote it before he was in the Quarry Men or The Beatles.

In Spite of All the Danger
(*Anthology*)

Written by Paul, with a guitar solo by George. Influenced by Elvis, it has two claims to fame. It was the embryonic Beatles' first record, made in 1958 in

Percy Phillips' small studio at 38 Kensington, Liverpool, for less than £1. Also, it was the only original song performed by the Quarry Men at that time. This historic event is marked by a plaque, one of a growing number initiated by fellow Liverpudlian Fred O'Brien.

Julia (*The Beatles*)

Although *Julia* was directed at his mother, John is also telling her that he has found a new love – 'ocean child' (Yoko in Japanese). As Paul said of Julia – "...John absolutely adored her, and not just because she was his mum." Written by John during his latter Beatle days, this gentle song couldn't be more different than *Mother*.

Like Dreamers Do (*Anthology*)

An early Paul number which became part of the Quarry Men's and then The Beatles' repertoire until 1962.

Love Me Do (*Please Please Me*)

Written by Paul whilst sagging off school. John's main contribution was the middle eight and the distinctive harmonica solo. John had played the mouth organ since childhood and had admired Delbert McClinton's harmonica work on Bruce Channel's *Hey Baby*. John was to meet him at the Tower Ballroom in New Brighton a few months before The Beatles recorded *Love Me Do* and Delbert generously showed him his technique. *Love Me Do* is also memorable because producer George Martin wasn't happy with new boy Ringo's drumming and replaced him on the recording with session drummer Andy White.

Maggie May (*Let It Be*)

The final 'throw-away' track on the *Let It Be* album, *Maggie May* is a well-known Liverpool folk song about a local prostitute who plied her trade along Lime Street, one of the main streets in the city centre (opposite page, above). The song was a hit for the Vipers during the mid-50's skiffle boom and formed part of the Quarry Men's repertoire.

Liverpool-Welsh playwrite Alun Owen, who's success with the play *No Trams To Lime Street*, led to him writing the screenplay for The Beatles' first film *A Hard Day's Night*, went on to write the musical *Maggie May* with composer Lionel Bart.

Michelle (*Rubber Soul*)

Largely written by Paul, the song had its origins in a party piece with which he amused his, and John's art college, friends. Jan Vaughan, the wife of Ivan Vaughan, who introduced his schoolfriend Paul McCartney to John Lennon, was a French teacher and helped Paul out with the lyrics, coming up with the girl's name – 'Michelle, ma belle' – and the line – 'sont les mots qui vont tres bien ensemble' ('These are words that go together well').

Mother
(*John Lennon/Plastic Ono Band*)

The opening song on John's solo album *John Lennon/Plastic Ono Band*. The song's gut-wrenching intensity is almost too painful to listen to. Julia was the mother he lost twice – once at the age of five when Julia handed him over to her sister Mimi to look after and again at the age of 17 when she was killed in a road accident outside Mimi's house. The song opens with the disquieting sound of a funeral church bell (church bells were rooted in John's childhood – "Sundays, I heard church bells") and ends with John screaming over and over again – "Mummy don't go. Daddy come home".

My Mummy's Dead
(*John Lennon/Plastic Ono Band*)

The closing song on John's debut solo album with the death of his beloved mother Julia again as its theme.

Norwegian Wood (*Rubber Soul*)

John said that he wrote this song about an affair he'd had whilst at the same time trying to prevent his wife Cynthia finding out about it. John's friend and fellow Quarry Man, Pete Shotton, thought that the song harked back to John's student days in the Gambier Terrace flat (top) he shared with Stu Sutcliffe, specifically the reference to sleeping in the bath and John's practice of burning wooden furniture in the fireplace.

One After 909 (*Let It Be*)

Written by John in 1957, probably in Paul's house at Forthlin Road. Paul elaborated: – We used to sag off school, go back to my house and the two of us would write. There are a lot of songs from back then that we've never reckoned on because they're all very unsophisticated songs…We hated the words to *One After 909*."

One-time Liverpool artist Maurice Cockrill R.A.'s interpretation of Penny Lane.

Penny Lane (*Magical Mystery Tour*)

Although John had first mentioned Penny Lane in the original draft of *In My Life*, it was Paul who wrote this nostalgic song. When Liverpudlians refer to 'Penny Lane' they mean the general area that has the Penny Lane 'roundabout' as its focus. Penny Lane itself is a narrow road that leads from the University of Liverpool's Halls of Residence at Greenbank to its junction with Smithdown Road and Allerton Road. For the first five years of his life John virtually lived in Penny Lane – his home was just around the corner in the family's house at 9 Newcastle Road.

Suburban and mundane though it may appear in real life, Penny Lane is a 'must see' for all Beatle fans visiting Liverpool. The barber's shop is still there although Mr Bioletti, the barber who gave John, Paul and George their 'short back and sides' haircuts when they were children, isn't. The bank is there too and so is the shelter in the middle of the roundabout. Originally a bus shelter, it was converted into *Sgt Pepper's Bistro*. Further along Allerton Road at its junction with Mather Avenue is the local fire station.

Explaining how the song was written,

John said – "It was just reliving childhood." Paul elaborated - "Penny Lane is a bus roundabout in Liverpool; and there is a barber's shop showing photographs of every head he's had the pleasure to know - no that's not true, they're just photos of hairstyles, but all the people who come and go stop and say hello. It's part fact, part nostalgia for a place which is a great place, blue suburban skies as we remember it, and it's still there."

Please Please Me (*Please Please Me*)

Many of John's musical influences came from his mother Julia and the songs she sang to him as a child. A

...and his take on Strawberry Field.

Bing Crosby hit in the early 30's, *Please* was one such song. A born wordsmith, John was intrigued with the line – 'Oh please, lend your little ears to my pleas.' and its twin meanings of the words 'please' and 'pleas'. *Please Please Me* was written by John in his bedroom at 251 Menlove Avenue (see opposite page). He recalled – "I remember the day and the pink eyelet on the bed." (he probably meant 'coverlet', a bed-spread). He'd also been influenced by Roy Orbison's *Only The Lonely* and pictured him singing *Please Please Me* – the original version of John's song was much slower.

Polythene Pam (Abbey Road)

Written and sung by John – "...I used a thick Liverpool accent because it was supposed to be about a mythical Liverpool scrubber dressed up in her jackboots and kilt."

There was in fact a young girl fan of the Beatles called Pat from their Cavern days who, unbelievably, had a bizarre habit of eating polythene. She was known to The Beatles as Polythene Pat. Subsequently, John claimed that the song related to an incident when a friend involved him in a threesome with a girl dressed in polythene!

PS I Love You (Please Please Me)

Mainly written by Paul with some help from John after Paul's girlfriend Dot Rhone visited him in Hamburg. Head over heels in love with Paul, she assumed that he had her in mind when writing this 1962 song, a supposition Paul later denied, explaining that he never had any specific girl in mind. Paul ended their relationship that summer at 93 Garmoyle Road, the flat she shared with John's girlfriend, Cynthia.

Step Inside Love (Anthology)

The Beatles' association with the Liverpool singer and entertainer Cilla Black stretched back to the days when she was a cloakroom attendant at the Cavern club. Fitting therefore that Paul should write this as the theme song for her new TV series *Cilla* in 1968. She also recorded two other songs – *Love of the Loved*, an old Quarry Men's song that became her first single, and Paul's *It's for You*.

Strawberry Fields Forever (Magical Mystery Tour)

John regarded this as his favourite Beatle song. Like Penny Lane, Strawberry Field (no 's' please!) is a real place close to where John lived in Menlove Avenue. In fact he could get there from his back garden. The wooded grounds of this Salvation Army children's home were familiar to John and his school-friends as they climbed trees and played hide and seek amongst the bushes.

Reputedly, although Paul has denied it, this was the first song on a new album that was to be autobiographical and would develop the Liverpool themes hinted at in songs such as *In My Life* and *Eleanor Rigby*. The concept was abandoned in favour of the Sgt Pepper album and *Strawberry Fields* and *Penny Lane* were issued as a single.

Strawberry Field also gets a mention on *Glass Onion* - "I told you about Strawberry Field. You know the place where nothing is real."

When I'm 64 (*Sgt. Pepper's Lonely Hearts Club Band*)

Written in the style of the 20's and 30's songs played by Paul's father in his days heading the Jim Mac Band, it was released when Paul's dad was 64. However, it was composed much earlier on the family piano in Forthlin Road when Paul was 16.

Working Class Hero
(*John Lennon/ Plastic Ono Band*)

John's cynical, world-weary song from his *Imagine* album is firmly grounded in his school and college days in Liverpool. Many people misunderstood the song and thought that John was referring to himself as the working class hero. In fact, John had been brought up in the green and genteel suburb of Woolton in a house that still has the buzzer system with which the master or mistress could summon the domestic help. Although his origins were undeniably working class, John's 'career' since the time he left art college was that of 'musician and artist'.

This Yellow Submarine has been part of the local scene since 1984. Currently, it welcomes visitors on arrival at Liverpool John Lennon Airport.

Yellow Submarine
(*Yellow Submarine*)

The title song of the Beatles' animated film was written by Paul as a children's song to be sung by Ringo. During visits to Merseyside when he had young children of his own, Paul and family would sing *Yellow Submarine* as they travelled under the river through the Mersey Tunnel.

The remixed songtrack and digitally enhanced film were premiered at the Philharmonic Hall, Liverpool, on 14th September 1999.

You'll Be Mine (*Anthology*)

Made in 1960 on a borrowed tape recorder in Paul's house (below), it is noteworthy only because it was the first recording of a Lennon and McCartney song.

The 'Don' to whom this signed 'Four Aces' photograph is dedicated is the writer's long-time friend, Don Andrew, former bass player with the Remo Four who shared the bill with The Beatles on many occasions. Apart from Ringo who plays it safe with 'Best Wishes', John quips 'Sodoffy from John Leper'. George signs his 'Geoff Harrison' and Paul, a class-mate of Don's at the Liverpool Institute, dedicates his 'from another fat schoolboy'.

INDIVIDUAL BEATLES
John
4, 10, 12, 13, 14, 15, 16, 21, 22, 23, 24, 26, 27, 30, 31, 32, 33, 34, 35, 36, 38, 39, 41, 44, 49, 51, 52, 55, 5, 57, 58, 59, 60, 62-72, 73, 74, 75, 80, 83, 87, 89, 92, 96, 97, 98, 99, 100, 101, 102, 103, 104, 105, 106.

Paul
4, 10, 11, 15, 16, 17, 19, 20, 21, 24, 25, 26, 28, 29, 30, 31, 32, 34, 38, 39, 40, 42, 45, 46, 47, 52, 55, 56, 57, 61, 62, 66, 68-69, 70, 71, 73-74, 75, 76, 77, 79, 80, 82, 83, 87, 88, 91, 92, 95, 96, 98, 99, 100, 101, 102, 103, 104, 105, 106.

George
14, 15, 19, 20, 21, 24, 26, 28, 29, 30, 31, 32, 39, 41, 45, 52, 55, 58, 59, 60, 61, 66, 71, 74, 76, 77, 80, 81, 87, 89, 92, 94, 96, 99.

Ringo
11, 15, 19, 31, 24, 25, 35, 36, 43, 46, 51-54, 80, 87, 90, 92, 96, 99, 106.

IN MY LIVERPOOL HOME - BEATLE HOUSES
John
9 Newcastle Road, 59, 60, 101, 104
'Mendips', 251 Menlove Avenue, 64, 89, 100, 100, 104, 105
3 Gambier Terrace, 33, 103

Paul
10 Sunbury Road, 80
72 Western Avenue, 75
12 Ardwick Road, 76
20 Forthlin Road, 66, 73, 76, 91, 98, 100, 103, 106

George
12 Arnold Grove, 60
25 Upton Green, 76
174 Mackets Lane, 71, 76

Ringo
9 Madryn Street, 51-52
10 Admiral Grove, 54

LESSON LEARNED - THE BEATLES' SCHOOLS AND COLLEGES
John
Mosspits Lane Primary School, 60
Dovedale Road Infants and Junior School, 58-59
Quarry Bank Grammar School (now Calderstones) 4, 32, 62, 66, 97, 100
Liverpool College of Art, 63, 97

Paul
Stockton Wood Primary School, 75
Liverpool Institute, 28-31, 76

George
Dovedale Road Infants and Junior School, 58-59
Liverpool Institute, 28-31, 76

Ringo
St Silas Church of England Primary School, 54
Dingle Vale Secondary Modern School, 54

BEATLE GIGS - VENUES
Aintree Institute, 92
Air Training Corps (ATC) Club, Birkdale, 94
Albany Cinema, Maghull, 92
Alexandra Hall, Crosby, 94
Barnston Women's Institute
Blair Hall, 92
Blue Angel, 35
Cabaret Club, 92
Cambridge Hall, Southport, 94
Casbah Coffee Club, 10, 81-83
Cassanova Club(s), 14, 17
Cavern, 6, 10, 16, 35, 40, 42, 44-47, 84, 105
Childwall Labour Club, 92
Clubmoor Conservative Men's Club / New Clubmoor Hall, 83
David Lewis Theatre, 92
Earlestown Town Hall, St Helens,
Ellesmere Port Civic Centre, South Wirral, 95
Empire Theatre, 17, 18-19, 85

Finch Lane Social Club, 92
Floral Hall, Southport, 94
Gateacre Labour Club, 93
Glenpark Club, Southport, 94
Grafton Ballroom, The, 79
Grosvenor Ballroom, 88
Haig Dance Club, Moreton, 95
Hambleton Hall, 93
Heswall Jazz Club, Wirral, 91
Holyoake Hall, 93
Hulme Hall, 90
Irby Village Hall, Wirral, - see Newton Dancing School
Iron Door Club, The, 14
Jacaranda Coffee Bar, 37-38
Kingsway Club, Southport, 95
Knotty Ash Village Hall, 93
Lathom Hall, 83
Lee Park Golf Club, 93
Lewis's store, 21
Litherland Town Hall, 84
Little Theatre, Southport, 94
Liverpool College of Art, 31-33
Liverpool Jazz Society, 14
Locarno Ballroom, The, 79
Lowlands club, 93
Macdona Hall, West Kirby, 90
Majestic Ballroom, Birkenhead, 56, 87, 88
Merseyside Civil Service Club, 92
Morgue Skiffle Cellar, 93
Mossway Hall, 93
Neston Institute, Wirral, 95
New Cabaret Artistes, 93
New Clubmoor Hall - see Clubmoor Conservative Men's Club
New Colony Club, 93
Newton Dancing School, Irby, 95
Odd Spot club, 36
Odeon Cinema, Liverpool, 13, 17
Odeon Cinema, Southport, 94
Pavilion Theatre, 93
Peppermint Lounge, 17
Picton Road Bus Depot Social Club, 93
Plaza Ballroom, St Helens, 94
Quarry Bank High School, (now Calderstones) 93

Queen's Hall, Widnes, 94
Queens Hotel, Southport, 95
Rialto Ballroom, 93
Rosebery Street, 93
Royal Iris cruiseship, 12
St Barnabas Church Hall, 57, 58
St John's Hall, Bootle, 94
St John's Hall, Tuebrook, 94
St Luke's Church Youth Club, Crosby, 94
St Paul's Presbyterian Church Hall, Tranmere, 95
St Peter's Church/Hall, 15, 69, 70-71
Stanley Abattoir Social Club,
Starline Club, 94
Technical College, Birkenhead, 95
Temple, The, 14,
Tower Ballroom, New Brighton, 89
Upton Green, 76
Victoria Hall, Higher Bebington, 95
Wilson Hall, 94
Winter Gardens ballroom, 94
Woolton Village Club, 94
Woolton Village Fete - see St Peter's Church / Hall
Wyvern Social Club - see Blue Angel
YMCA, Birkenhead, 95
YMCA, Hoylake, 95

IN THE FOOTSTEPS OF THE BEATLES - STREETS

Admiral Grove, 54
Aigburth Vale, 55
Allerton Road, 72
Ardwick Road, 76
Arnold Grove, 60
Back Broadway, 83
Banks Road, West Kirby, 91
Baskervyle Road, Heswall, 74, 91, 99
Beaconsfield Road, 63
Beatle Streets: John Lennon Drive, Paul McCartney Way, George Harrison Close, Ringo Starr Close, Epstein Court, Apple Court, Cavern Court, 80
Blomfield Road, 60, 71-72, 97
Bold Street, 4, 36, 38
Church Road, 101
Conway Street, Birkenhead, 87

Damwood Road, 76
Dingle Vale, 55
Dovedale Road, 58, 60, 61
Duke Street, 35
Falkner Street, 26, 98
Forthlin Road, 66, 73, 76, 91, 98, 100, 103, 106
Gambier Terrace, 33, 103
Garmoyle Road, 56, 105
Grosvenor Street, Wallasey, 88
Hanover Street, 38
Harrington Street, 42
Harthill Road, 62
Hatton Hill Road, 84
Hayman's Green, 81
High Park Street, 54
Hope Street, 24
Kensington Fields, 80
Lathom Avenue, 83
Lime Street, 103
Long Lane, 81
Lord Street, 39, 42
Mackets Lane, 71, 76
Madryn Street, 51-52
Mathew Street, 7, 42-47
Menlove Avenue, 64, 89, 100, 100, 104, 105
Mosspits Lane, 60
Mount Street, 28
Naylorsfield Drive, 76
Newcastle Road, 59, 60, 101, 104
North Mossley Hill Road, 71
North John Street, 42, 48
Oxford Street, 23
Parker Street, 39
Pengwern Street, 54
Penny Lane, 56-57, 101, 105
Percy Street, 33
Rainford Gardens, 42, 43
Rainford Square, 42, 43
Renshaw Street, 36
Rice Lane, 80
Rice Street, 27
Rodney Street, 22
Salisbury Avenue, West Kirby, 91
School Lane, 39
Shaw Street, 79
Slater Street, 37
Speke Road, 74
Stanley Road, 94
Stanley Street, 41
Stockton Wood Road, 75
Sunbury Road, 80
Trinity Road, Hoylake, 89
Upton Green, 76
West Derby Road, 79
Western Avenue, 75

PEOPLE IN THEIR LIVES

Andrew, Don, 29
Aspinall, Neil,, 29, 43
Ballard, Arthur, 31, 33
Barker, Clive, 59
Bart, Lionel, 103
Berry, Chuck, 45
Best, Mona, 81, 82
Best, Pete, 66, 79, 81-83, 89
Big Three, 17, 46, 53, 91
Black, Cilla, 35, 46, 53, 81, 105
Blackjacks, 81
Blake, Peter, 16, 48
Blundell, Bryan, 39
Bron, Eleanor, 98
Brown, Joe & his Bruvvers, 89
Brown, Ken, 83
Caldwell, Iris, 101
Carroll, Lewis, 100
Cass & The Cassanovas, 14, 35, 46
Chadwick, Les, 37
Chang, Barry, 38
Churchill, Winston, 23
Clague, Police Constable, 67
Clan McLeod Pipe Band, 89
Cole Porter, 100
Crawford, Marie (née Maguire), 25
Crosby, Bing, 65, 105
Curtis, Lee & The All Stars, 89
Davey, Joe, 35
Davis, Carl, 26, 34
Decker, Thomas, 99
Del Vikings, 68
Delaney & Bonnie, 19
Delaney, Eric, 25
Delaney, Paddy, 6
Dissenters, The, 27
Donegan, Lonnie, 45
Dooley, Arthur, 44
Dorn, Beno, 91
Doubleday, John, 47
Douglas, Craig, 18
Dykins, John (Bobby), 36, 56, 59, 71, 72
Dylan, Bob, 35
Disney, 98
Eaton, Bob, 24
Eddie Clayton Skiffle Group, 53
Ellis, Royston, 27
Elmes, Harvey Lonsdale, 19
Epstein, Brian, 10, 20, 21, 22, 26, 27, 36, 38, 39, 41, 46, 61, 62, 66, 81, 82, 84, 87, 91, 98
Epstein, Harry & Queenie, 22, 61

Indexes

Epstein, Jacob, 21
Evans, Mike, 16
Fourmost, The, 46, 100
Garland, Judy, 35
Garry, Len, 29
Gentle, Johnny, 20, 35, 83, 87
Gerry & The Pacemakers, 11, 12, 44, 46, 53, 88
Ginsberg, Allen, 24
Graves, Harry, 52, 53
Gregson, John, 27
Gretty, Jim, 41
Haley, Bill, 17
Harrison, Peter, 76
Harry, Bill, 11, 27, 36, 87, 88
Hendrix, Jimmy, 45
Hogarth, Geoff, 14
Holly, Buddy & The Crickets, 25, 45, 100
Hope, Bob, 100
Horne, Rowena, 57
Hughes, David, 43
Hutchinson, Johnny, 35
Jackson, Mike, 14
Jet Harris, 18
Johnny & The Moondogs, 18
Johnson, Arthur, 44
Jolier, Vincent, 99
Jones, Raymond, 40
Jung, Carl Gustav, 24
Kaye, Peter (alias Bill Connell), 36, 37
Kelly, Brian, 84
Kirchherr, Astrid, 16, 55
Kramer, Billy J, 27, 44, 98
Lauper, Cyndi, 12
Leach, Sam, 14, 17, 89
Lennon, Cynthia, 10, 11, 16, 21, 26, 27, 31, 33, 39, 47, 55, 56, 57, 66, 83, 89, 97, 98, 100, 103, 105
Lennon, Freddie, 22, 23, 55, 59
Lennon, Julia, 10, 14, 22, 23, 36, 55, 56, 59, 67, 71, 72, 102, 103, 104
Lennon, Julian, 20, 55, 56, 57, 66, 89, 100
Lennon, Sean, 21, 33, 43
Levis, Carroll, 18
Little Richard, 18, 87, 89
Lynch, Kenny, 18
Martin, George. 11, 20, 26, 30, 43, 102
Mason, Ann, 33
Maury, James, 22
McCartney, Jim, 73, 74, 75, 80, 91, 99, 106
McCartney, Linda, 73
McCartney, Mary, 73, 75, 80
McCartney, Mike, 28, 47, 57,

73, 74, 75, 80
McClinton, Delbert, 102
McFall, Ray, 46
McGann, Mark, 24
Miles, Ed, 53
Mimi, Aunt, 23, 33, 59, 62, 65, 67, 71, 73, 103
Murphy, Tom, 75
Murray, Rod, 27, 33, 34
Mynogue, Kylie, 12
NEMS (North End Music Store), 20, 22, 40, 46
O'Brien, Fred, 102
Olmstead, Frederick, 64
Ono, Yoko, 4, 12, 21, 26, 32, 33, 39, 59, 63, 64, 66, 75, 102
Orbison, Roy, 105
Owen, Alun, 103
Paolozzi, Eduardo, 11, 16, 55
Parnes, Larry, 35
Paxton, Joseph, 64
Peters, Mark & The Cyclones, 17
Phillips, Percy, 102
Pobjoy, Ernest, 63
Powell, Cynthia - see 'Lennon, Cynthia'
Pytka, Joe, 99
Quarry Men, 18, 45, 57, 58, 62, 63, 68-69, 70, 71, 74, 76, 79, 81, 83, 101, 102, 103, 105
Queen Elizabeth, 16, 30, 71
Reed, Lou, 12
Remo Four, 29, 46
Rhone, Dot, 56, 105
Roberts, Margaret, 37
Rolling Stones, 26, 35, 45
Rowe, Dick, 26
Royal Caribbean steel band, 37, 38
Roza, Lita, 44
Rushworth, James, 41
Russell, Willy, 24
Searchers, The, 46
Sellers, Peter, 17
Shannon, 48
Shotton, Pete, 101, 103
Silver Beatles,
Silver Beats, 83
Sissons, Peter, 59
Sounds Incorporated, 18
Starkey, Elsie, 51, 52, 53
Starkey, Zak, 19
Steele, Tommy, 43
Storm, Rory & The Hurricanes, 17, 35, 46, 53, 101
Sutcliffe, Stuart, 11, 15-16, 19, 27, 32, 33, 34, 35, 38,

39, 55, 83, 84, 89, 101, 103
Swinging Blue Jeans, The, 46
Tarbuck, Jimmy, 59
Taylor, Teddy (Kingsize) 14
Travis, Randy, 12
Vaughan, Ivan and Jan, 70, 103
Vipers, 103
Washington, George, 22
Whalley, Nigel, 67
White, Andy, 102
Whitty, Mark Featherstone, 30
Who, The, 45
Wilde, Oscar, 4
Williams, Allan, 11, 17, 19, 35, 37, 38, 46, 88
Wilson, Sir Harold, 46
Wings, 19, 20, 46
Wooler, Bob, 17, 36, 40, 46, 62, 84
Woodbine, Lord, 38
Young, Phil, 44

LITERARY LIVERPOOL - SONGS, BOOKS, FILMS ETC WITH A BEATLES / LIVERPOOL CONNECTION

A Hard Day's Night, 11, 13, 17, 103
A Spaniard in the Works, 62, 98
Abbey Road, 99, 105
Anthology, 82, 98, 100, 101, 102, 105, 106
Backbeat, 17
Ballroom Dancing, 79
Be Bop A Lula, 70
Bedtime for Drums, 25
Beatles For Sale, 100
Blackbird Singing, 24
Cayenne, 98
Come Go With Me, 68, 70
Cumberland Gap, 70
Daily Howl, 62
Do You Want to Know a Secret?, 27, 89
Eleanor Rigby, 43, 98, 99, 106
Flaming Pie, 36
Free As A Bird, 99
Give My Regards to Broad Street, 17, 79
Glass Onion, 99, 100, 106
God, 100
Golden Slumbers, 99
Guitar Boogie, 83
Heartbreak Hotel, 65
Hello Little Girl, 65, 100
Help, 98
Hey Baby, 102

Hey Jude, 100
I Am The Walrus, 99, 100
I Call Your Name, 65, 101
I Lost My Little Girl, 100
I Saw Her Standing There, 73, 101
I'll Follow The Sun, 100
I'll Get You, 100
In His own Write, 62
In My Life, 101, 104, 106
In Spite of All The Danger, 101
It's De-lovely, 100
It's For You, 105
John Lennon/Plastic Ono Band, 103, 106
John Paul George Ringo and Bert, 24
Julia, 67, 102
Lennon, 24
Lennon: A Tribute, 13
Let It Be, 103
Like Dreamers Do, 102
Liverpool Oratorio, 26, 34
Liverpool 8, 19, 53
Love Me Do, 73, 82, 89, 102
Love of the Loved, 105
Maggie May, 20, 70, 102, 103
Magical Mystery Tour, 100, 104, 105
Maybe Baby, 100
Mersey Beat newspaper, 4,10, 23, 36, 40, 87, 88
Michelle, 103
Mother, 67, 102, 103
My Anthology, 100, 199
My Bonnie, 40
My Mummy's Dead, 103
No Trams To Lime Street, 103
Norwegian Wood, 103
One After 909, 65, 103
Only The Lonely, 65, 105
Past Masters: Vol 1, 100, 101
Penny Lane, 57, 104, 105, 106
Please Please Me, 27, 79, 98, 101, 102, 104-105
Polythene Pam, 105
PS I Love You, 105
Railroad Bill, 70
Revolver, 98
Rubber Soul, 101, 103
Run Devil Run, 26
Sgt Pepper, 16, 106
Sgt Pepper's Magical Mystery Trip, 24
She Loves You, 100
Snow White & The Seven Dwarfs, 98
Something New, 11

Sport, Speed & Illustrated, 58
Standing Stone, 26
Step Inside Love, 105
Strawberry Field, 63-64, 99, 105, 106
The 1 Album, 100
The Beatles, 99, 102
The Magic Christian, 17
The Walrus & The Carpenter, 100
Through The Looking Glass, 100
Twenty Flight Rock, 70
Twist of Lennon, 10
Walls & Bridges, 58
When I'm 64, 106
Working Class Hero, 106
Working Classical, 26
Yellow Submarine, 26, 99, 106, 107
You'll Be Mine, 106

STATUES, SCULPTURES, PLAQUES ETC
Cavern Quarter:
-   Arthur Dooley's sculpture, 44
-   David Hughes' sculpture, 43
-   Wall of Fame, 44
-   Wall of Hits, 44
-   John Doubleday's statue, 47
-   Tommy Steele's statue of Eleanor Rigby, 43
-   John Lennon statue, 46
-   Plaque marking entrance to original Cavern club, 47
-   Bob Wooler plaque, 46
-   Grapes pub plaque, 44
Casbah Coffee Club plaque, 83
Dissenters plaque, 27
Grosvenor Ballroom, Wallasey, plaque, 88
Iron Door Club plaque, 14
Jacaranda club plaque, 37
John Lennon's birthplace plaque, 23
John and Paul meet for the first time - plaque at St Peter's Church Hall, 74
Liverpool John Lennon Airport - Tom Murphy's John Lennon statue, 75
Liverpool Town Hall Freedom of the City inscription, 13
'Mendips', 251 Menlove Avenue, English Heritage blue plaque for John, 66

Peace Garden (memorial trees for John and George), 14
Quarry Men plaque, 102

MISCELLANEOUS
Art of The Beatles exhibition, 16, 31
Bag One, 16, 33
Beatle Club, 91
Beatlemania, 84
Beatles Convention, 20, 82
Beatles Story, 10, 13
Butlins, 53
Cavern City Tours, 47
Dockers' umbrella - see 'Overhead Railway'
Eiffel Tower, 89
Elmswood Nursing Home, 71
English Heritage, 66, 74
Ferry 'cross the Mersey, 41
Freemen of Liverpool, 13, 15, 17
Green Goddess, 12
Hannay, A & Co, 75
Jim Mac's Band, 106
John Moores Liverpool Exhibition, 15
Juke Box Jury, 18
Lancashire & Cheshire Beat Group Competition, 26
Lennon's Liverpool - Top Ten sights, 97
Liver Birds, 12
Liverpool Cotton Exchange, 73
Liverpool Echo
Magical Mystery Tour bus
Mathew Street Festival, 47
National Trust, 66, 73
Northern Area Fan Club, 18
Operation Big Beat, 89
Overhead Railway, 12, 101
Poole, 65
Radio Luxembourg, 65
Royal Life, 47
Royal Liverpool Philharmonic Orchestra, 34
Salvation Army, 63, 106
Statues, sculptures, plaques etc - see separate index
The Rebels, 76
Top Rank, 87
University of Liverpool, 13, 26, 104
Yellow submarine, 75

IMAGE CREDITS

Don Andrew – 107

Pete Best – 83 (centre)

The late Bill Connell (Peter Kaye) – 3, 18 (bottom), 36 (bottom), 41 (centre), 46 (centre), 51 (top and circled), 54 (bottom), 80 (circled), 94 (bottom), 93 (bottom right).

Maurice Cockrill – 104 (top), 105 (top)

EMI Records Ltd – 64 (inset)

Leslie Kearney – 95 (top)

Liverpool Echo – 12 (bottom), 13, (bottom right), 90 (top).

The Mersey Partnership – Visitor Map, inside back cover.

Mike McCready – Front cover (Beatles)

Ann Mason – 38 (top right)

National Trust - 65 (top right), 66 (top right), 74. *These digital images are the property of NTPL and are protected by copyright.*

Geoff Rhind – 68-69

Geoff Roberts - 26 (right)

The late Graham Spencer – 88 (bottom)

Don Valentine – 31 (top), 90 (top)

With the exception of a small number of photographs whose ownership is not known to me (I would be pleased to give due acknowledgement in future editions), all other images are from the collection of the author.

All location photographs are the copyright of Ron Jones.